AFRICAN LAW
New Law For New Nations

Titles published in
The Library of Law and Contemporary Problems

POPULATION CONTROL, The Imminent World Crisis
MELVIN G. SHIMM, *Editor*, (and others)

EUROPEAN REGIONAL COMMUNITIES,
A New Era on the Old Continent
MELVIN G. SHIMM, *Editor*, (and others)

AFRICAN LAW, New Law for New Nations
HANS W. BAADE, *Editor*, (and others)

AFRICAN LAW
New Law For New Nations

HANS W. BAADE, *Editor*

ROBINSON O. EVERETT, *Associate Editor*

OCEANA PUBLICATIONS, INC.
Dobbs Ferry, New York
1963

© Copyright, 1963, by Duke University

Library of Congress Catalog Card Number 63-17558

Originally Published in Autumn 1962

by

LAW AND CONTEMPORARY PROBLEMS
DUKE UNIVERSITY SCHOOL OF LAW

PRINTED IN THE UNITED STATES OF AMERICA

TABLE OF CONTENTS

FOREWORD 1
    Hans W. Baade

**AFRICAN LEGAL STUDIES—A SURVEY OF THE FIELD
    AND THE ROLE OF THE UNITED STATES** 9
    Denis V. Cowen

**PERSONNEL PROBLEMS IN THE ADMINISTRATION OF
    JUSTICE IN NIGERIA** 41
    Sir Adetokunbo Ademola

**THE EVOLUTION OF GHANA LAW SINCE
    INDEPENDENCE** 47
    William Burnett Harvey

CUSTOMARY LAW IN THE NEW AFRICAN STATES 71
    Lloyd Fallers

**THE FUTURE OF ISLAMIC LAW IN BRITISH
    COMMONWEALTH TERRITORIES IN AFRICA** 83
    J. N. D. Anderson

**UNITED NATIONS LAW IN AFRICA: THE CONGO
    OPERATION AS A CASE STUDY** 99
    Thomas M. Franck

FOREWORD

A little knowledge is a dangerous thing. When the Editor invited Professor J. N. D. Anderson to contribute an article on Islamic Law in Africa to the present symposium, he indicated that in his judgment, discussion should focus on two points which—to him—seemed to merit special attention, to wit: (1) whether a modern society can long remain viable if it has an interpersonal conflict of laws system; (2) whether a revealed divine law is or can be rendered sufficiently adaptable for the purposes of resolving the typical conflicts of an industrial society. With obliging candor, Professor Anderson starts off his paper by observing that these two questions are not infrequently asked "by those who approach the subject ... with a general idea as to the nature of (Islamic) law but a limited acquaintance with legal developments, during the last century or more, in the Middle East, the Indian subcontinent, and the dependent or formerly dependent territories of East and West Africa."[1]

Professor Anderson's contribution convincingly demonstrates that the two issues singled out by the Editor are neither unique to Africa, nor as important as is often assumed, nor finally really detrimental to national advance in the African states. The same observation can probably be made about most other legal problems currently arising in the new African states. It would seem, therefore, that the uniqueness of African legal problems does not primarily lie in the—at least to Western observers—unusual and frequently archaic character of major legal institutions to be found in the various African states. It is, rather, the clash between a truly singular cumulation of such institutions and an equally unprecedented pressure for the speedy attainment of modernity that makes African legal problems so unique.

If the above observations are correct, much of what has been written about African law by comparative and international lawyers will require a careful re-examination. This would appear to be especially the case with respect to attempts to deduce "general principles of law"[2] from various African legal institutions. For instance, the discussion of various African tribal laws in C. Wilfred Jenks' *Common Law of Mankind* (the most ambitious effort so far in the direction of establishing a world legal system by comparative research) would appear to rely largely on those institutions which—not necessarily typical to Africa but fairly often witnessed in traditional, pre-industrial societies—are among the first to be swept away by the tide of

---

[1] Anderson, *The Future of Islamic Law in British Commonwealth Territories in Africa, infra* p. 617.
[2] See generally Schlesinger, *Research on the General Principles of Law Recognized by Civilized Nations*, 51 AM. J. INT'L L. 734 (1957); *id., The Common Core of Legal Systems: An Emerging Subject for Comparative Study*, XXTH CENTURY COMPARATIVE AND CONFLICTS LAW (LEGAL ESSAYS IN HONOR OF HESSEL E. YNTEMA) 65 (1961).

modernity.[3] Learned references to Ashanti "constitutional" law fade into insignificance when confronted with the hard facts of the constitution of Ghana.[4] The same observations seemingly appear with at least equal force to present attempts to establish universal legal rules in favor of the status quo—such as the "sanctity" of contracts—on the basis of traditional or divine law.[5] One might well doubt the historical validity of such research. It seems, for instance, hard to believe that capitulations, Mixed Courts, and the introduction of Western law were really misguided acts by the colonial powers because Islamic law as actually in operation afforded all the security and justice needed. But quite aside from this; it appears abundantly clear that especially in the areas of law to which such studies apply (contracts, commercial law, public law), traditional law has been or is being rapidly swept away by Western-type institutions. And it seems rather difficult to unearth many "general principles" in the steadily crumbling bulwarks of traditional or religious law: status, family, and succession.

This is not to say that the new African states hold nothing of interest to students of comparative and international law. It is merely suggested that studies which focus on traditional and religious legal institutions are highly prone to be misleading or even mischievous—misleading because the institutions referred to are on the periphery even now and are rapidly melting away; mischievous because any emphasis on traditional or divine law necessarily poses ideological obstacles to the legal reforms which the African states must undertake in order to attain modernity.

Let us now turn to some practical examples. In the field of international law, for instance, it is submitted that little can be gained from scanning frequently obscure tribal and religious customs for evidence of "general principles of law." The new African states accept international law; several of them are currently before the International Court of Justice as plaintiffs against "white" powers.[6] They do not challenge the legal force of treaties concluded by free negotiation after independence. But they do worry about the status of pre-independence treaty obligations entered into by the colonial power; and they do object to the unilateral imposition of quite frequently disputed rules of customary international law which they did not help develop.[7]

Is such an attitude towards international law really to any appreciable extent the manifestation of a unique law-culture? It seems much more sensible to assume that at least as regards customary international law, the new African states are

[3] See, e.g., C. WILFRED JENKS, THE COMMON LAW OF MANKIND 91, 126, 127-28 (1958), but cf. id. at 112. For criticism, see especially Stone, *A Common Law of Mankind?*, I INTERNATIONAL STUDIES 414 (India 1960).
[4] See JENKS, op. cit. supra note 3, at 128; F.A.R. BENNION, THE CONSTITUTION OF GHANA (1962); LESLIE RUBIN & PAULI MURRAY, THE CONSTITUTION AND GOVERNMENT OF GHANA (1961).
[5] As exemplified by Habachy, *Property, Right, and Contract in Muslim Law*, 62 COLUM. L. REV. 450 (1962).
[6] The South West Africa Cases (Ethiopia and Liberia v. South Africa), Preliminary Objections, 1962 I.C.J. Reports 319; Case Concerning the Northern Cameroons (Cameroun v. United Kingdom), cf. Order of April 25, 1962, 1962 I.C.J. Reports 3.
[7] See Anand, *Rôle of the "New" Asian-African Countries in the Present International Legal Order*, 56 AM. J. INT'L L. 383 (1962); and Stone, *supra* note 3.

merely assuming the position indicated by the present stage of their economic development and by their national ambitions. They seek to avoid, or at any rate to minimize, the constraints imposed by an international custom which was created almost entirely by the capital-exporting countries.[8]

With respect to treaties, we seem to be faced by a series of "typical" cases of state succession, with, however, the distinguishing mark that the problem has not arisen until now with such pressing force and on such a large scale. It is estimated, for instance, that there are some 300-odd British treaties which might be applicable to Nigeria. By exchange of letters between the Prime Minister of the Federation of Nigeria and the United Kingdom High Commissioner on the very day of independence, the Federation Government assumed all rights and obligations stipulated by international agreements entered into "on their behalf" before independence, and undertook to keep such agreements in force "until such time as the Government of Nigeria can consider whether they require modification or renegotiation in any respect."[9] Nigeria was faced with three major questions in this connection: Which agreements are applicable to Nigeria? (For a country which has just reached independence and is still in the process of setting up a Foreign Office, this is no mean question.) Will the other contracting parties regard themselves to be bound as against Nigeria? How can the various agreements be denounced, and which agreements should be terminated?

Another new African state, Tanganyika, has attempted a different solution of the treaty problem. Instead of concluding an "inheritance agreement" with the United Kingdom, Tanganyika has filed a formal declaration with the Secretary General of the United Nations. Pursuant to this declaration, all valid bilateral treaties are kept in force on the basis of reciprocity for a trial period of two years, pending negotiations as to eventual readjustments. Multilateral treaties are to be dealt with by *ad hoc* agreements but Tanganyika undertakes to treat such agreements "as being in force vis-à-vis other States who rely on them in their relations with Tanganyika."[10]

Both solutions are seemingly unexceptionable under traditional international law. Since almost all relevant agreements can be terminated unilaterally by appropriate, relatively short-term notice, the essential legal problem is the question as to the extent of the other parties' obligation toward the new states. Vastly more complicated is the issue of the legality of pre-independence agreements between the former colonial powers and the emerging African states on the eve of independence.

As a rule, the former colonial power will seek guarantees in three distinct fields: the continued recognition of pre-independence obligations of the colonial administration, particularly of civil service tenure and pension rights;[11] the continued pro-

---

[8] See Friedmann, *The Changing Dimensions of International Law*, 62 COLUM. L. REV. 1147, 1151 (1962).

[9] Quoted by Cole, *The Independence Constitution of Federal Nigeria*, in ROBERT O. TILMAN & R. TAYLOR COLE (EDS.), THE NIGERIAN POLITICAL SCENE 63, 66 (1962). See also *id.* at 77-78.

[10] See Note, *Problem of State Succession in Africa: Statement of the Prime Minister of Tanganyika*, 11 INT'L & COMP. L. Q. 1210, 1211-12 (1962).

[11] See SIR CHARLES JEFFRIES, THE TRANSFER OF POWER (1961); KENNETH YOUNGER, THE PUBLIC SERVICE IN NEW STATES (1960).

tection of minorities—not necessarily European subjects—whom the colonial powers had undertaken to protect against the dominant local ethnic or religious groups; and finally, the continued preferential treatment of the former colonial power and its nationals, especially in matters of trade, investment, and the like.

While such guarantees, or some of them, could be incorporated into the independence constitutions enacted by the colonial power, such constitutional protection had already proved to be insufficient. For once independence was attained, the former dependency could—as the Union of South Africa eventually did—[12]repeal or amend its constitution. Even the abolition of an "unamendable" constitutional provision by revolutionary action would not be a violation of international law, as international law does not guarantee the constitutional form of sovereign states.

In their search for more abiding securities, at least two European powers—France and Belgium—turned to the novel expedient of a *pre*-independence *international* agreement with the emerging nations. The Loi fondamentale of the Congo, enacted in the form of a Belgian statute of May 19, 1960, provided in its article 49 that even before independence, the Government of the Congo could conclude a general treaty of friendship, assistance, and cooperation with Belgium, as well as particular conventions on the details of post-independence cooperation within the framework of such a treaty.[13] A "treaty" was actually concluded between Belgium and the Congo (as represented by its future government) before independence; it was promptly renounced when the Republic of the Congo became independent.[14]

The second example of a pre-independence agreement is the Evian Agreement between France and the Algerian National Liberation Front (F.L.N.), announced on March 18, 1962.[15] As early as September 19, 1958, the F.L.N. had formed a Provisional Government of the Algerian Republic. Between 1958 and the Evian negotiations, this government had been recognized, either *de iure* or *de facto*, by some 25 states. France had consistently treated such acts of recognition as "unfriendly acts," and had also consistently denied the legal existence of an Algerian government. On the day after the Evian settlement, the Soviet Union extended *de iure* recognition to the Provisional Government of the Algerian Republic. The French Foreign Minister summoned the Soviet Ambassador the same evening, informing him that neither the cease-fire nor the Evian Agreement had modified the legal status of Algeria, and that France would exercise both internal and external Algerian sovereignty until the self-determination plebiscite. When the Soviet Union failed

---

[12] For a comprehensive discussion of the various phases of process, see EDWARD MCWHINNEY, JUDICIAL REVIEW IN THE ENGLISH-SPEAKING WORLD 98-108, 190-99 (2d ed. 1960).

[13] Loi fondamentale relative aux structures du Congo, [1960] MONITEUR BELGE 3988, 3992. The expression used is "conclure" (in the Flemish text, "sluiten"), from which it seems to follow that approval by the Chambers as provided for by Art. 25, sec. 2, was not necessary. In any event, Article 25—if it follows dominant Belgian opinion on the subject—requires the approval of the Chambers merely for the internal effectiveness ("effet"), not the international validity of treaties.

[14] See Franck, *United Nations Law in Africa: The Congo Operation as a Case Study, infra,* p. 632, at 633, with note 1.

[15] For an English translation of the Evian Agreements, see 1 AMERICAN SOCIETY OF INTERNATIONAL LAW, INTERNATIONAL LAW MATERIALS 214 (1962).

to react to this announcement, the French Ambassador in Moscow was recalled.[16]

Here, we seem to have the unique case of the obligor admitting his capacity to contract, but the obligee denying it. One should ordinarily suppose that France would be hard put to affirm Algeria's capacity to contract at the time of the Evian Agreement, and that Algeria would be equally embarrassed in asserting that the Provisional Government of the Algerian Republic was at that time legally inexistent. Yet, obviously, neither side relied on the representations of the other, and there was in all probability no estoppel as to either.

Are these pre-independence agreements valid treaties? It seems that the Belgian treaty was a case of self-dealing pure and simple, as the Congolese government—before independence the creature of Belgian legislation—was accorded "international capacity" solely for the purpose of concluding this treaty. As an act of direct and delegated Belgian sovereignty, the treaty could outlive Congolese independence only if ratified in some form by the Republic of the Congo. On the other hand, the Evian Agreement was concluded with a government which was anything but the creature of France. It seems more appropriate to disregard French official denials of the legal existence of the Algerian government as mere political declarations, and to concede at least *de facto* authority to the latter government as of March, 1962.

In actual fact, the Belgian-Congolese treaty was denounced after independence; the French-Algerian agreement was not only approved by the Algerian plebiscite, but also by the new Algerian government. It remains to be seen whether these two cases will come to be regarded as precedents for pre-independence international agreements, a species of treaty born in Africa. In any event, however, the African states concerned were but reluctant partners in this attempt to develop new rules of international law.

Our conclusion, then, is that there is at least at the present no typically African school of thought in public international law, as contrasted with, say, Latin American doctrine. But what about constitutional law? Is it possible to find specific African ideas in the constitutions of the new African states? This would certainly seem to be the case at least to the limited extent that the new constitutions preserve tribal symbols and institutions, especially chieftaincy. On the whole, however, there seems little doubt that the new African constitutions draw their inspirations primarily from three European sources: Belgium, France, and Britain (the latter, usually *via* the "written" constitutions of India and Australia, and the British North America Act). Indeed, to an outside observer, the two most striking phenomena in African public law are not novel indigenous institutions, but first of all, the amazing

---

[16] The above description follows Rousseau, *Chronique des faits internationaux*, 66 REVUE GÉNÉRALE DE DROIT INTERNATIONAL PUBLIC 580, 623-32 (1962). See generally MOHAMMED BEDJAOUI, LAW AND THE ALGERIAN REVOLUTION (1961); THOMAS OPPERMANN, DIE ALGERISCHE FRAGE (1959); Flory, *Algérie et droit international*, 5 ANNUAIRE FRANÇAIS DE DROIT INTERNATIONAL 817 (1959); *id.*, *Algérie Algérienne et droit international*, 6 *id.* 972 (1960); *id.*, *Négociation ou dégagement en Algérie*, 7 *id.* 836 (1961); Charpentier, *La France et le G.P.R.A.*, *id.* at 855.

variation in the application of imported models, and secondly the curious lack of contagion of United States constitutional law.

The former phenomenon is most strikingly illustrated by the contrast between President Kasavubu's dismissal of Patrice Lumumba as Premier of the Republic of the Congo, and the dismissal of Chief Akintola, the Premier of the Western Region of Nigeria, by the Governor of that Region.

The Kasavubu-Lumumba crisis turned on the interpretation of article 22 of the Loi fondamentale which provides: "Le chef de l'Etat nomme et révoque le Premier Ministre et les Ministres." Did this really mean, as it literally seems to imply, that the Chief of State can dismiss the Prime Minister at will? This would appear to depend not so much on the wording of article 22 as on the basic characteristics of the institutions of Chief of State and Premier under the Loi fondamentale. Here, the constitutional lawyer would in all probability commence with an investigation of the proceedings of the constitutional convention, in this case, the Round Table Conference held in Brussels in January and February, 1960. He would establish that the Conference rejected a United States-type presidency and decided in favor of a non-political Chief of State, as in Belgium—with, of course, the thought that this position might conceivably be offered by the grateful Congolese people to the King of the Belgians.[17] A comparison between the Loi fondamentale and the Belgian constitution of 1831 would then establish that the former is (at least with respect to the institutions here material) an attempt to re-codify Belgian constitutional law and convention as it stood in 1960. The relevance of Belgian models, if at all in doubt, would be definitely settled by article 51, section 2 of the Loi fondamentale which provides that the Congolese Parliament can request binding interpretations of the Loi fondamentale from the Belgian parliament—a seemingly senseless provision if the latter is not to be guided by Belgian experience.

At this point the inquiry would be conveniently narrowed down to the question whether under Belgian constitutional law as it stood in 1960, the King could dismiss a Premier who had not demonstrably lost the confidence of Parliament. The answer seems quite clear: he could not.[18]

It is common knowledge that the Kasavubu-Lumumba crisis was not approached by any of the protagonists along the lines sketched above—or, for that matter, any other essentially legal line. But that is precisely what happened in the similar though fortunately somewhat less sanguinary constitutional crisis of the Western Region of Nigeria.

Here, there had been a major rift in the Government party, and 66 of the 124 members of the Region's Assembly had written a letter to the Governor, stating that the Premier no longer enjoyed their confidence. The Governor thereupon denied

---

[17] See FRANÇOIS PERIN, LES INSTITUTIONS POLITIQUES DU CONGO INDEPENDANT AU 30 JUIN 1960, at 27-29 (1960); Debbasch, *Le problème constitutionnel congolais*, [1962] REVUE DU DROIT PUBLIC 25, 41-42.

[18] 2 PIERRE WIGNY, DROIT CONSTITUTIONNEL 609-12 (1952); Debbasch, *supra* note 17, at 42-43. Article 65 of the Belgian constitution provides, in terms literally as unconditional as those of article 22 of the Loi fondamentale: "Le Roi nomine et révoque ses ministres."

to grant a dissolution to the Premier, dismissed him, and appointed a new Premier in his stead. Chief Akintola, the ousted Premier, challenged his removal from office in an action before the High Court of the Western Region of Nigeria. That court referred the constitutional questions raised by the action to the Federal Supreme Court.

The controversy centered on section 33(10)(a) of the constitution of the Western Region of Nigeria which provides that the Premier holds office at the Governor's pleasure, but that the Governor shall not remove the Premier "unless it appears to him that the Premier no longer commands the support of the majority of the members of the House of Assembly."[19] The questions posed in the referral were whether the Governor could remove the Premier (1) in the absence of a decision or resolution of no confidence, regularly adopted in the Assembly; or (2) on the basis of any materials extraneous to the proceedings of the Assembly.

Speaking for the majority of the Federal Supreme Court, Ademola, C.J.F., answered the first question in the negative, thereby deciding the issue in favor of plaintiff. He interpreted section 33(10) in the light of constitutional conventions obtaining in the United Kingdom and came to the conclusion that "Law and convention cannot be replaced by party political moves outside the House." The dissenting justice, Brett, F.J., agreed with the premise that United Kingdom constitutional convention was highly relevant to the issue. He found, however, that there was no constitutional precedent exactly in point, and consequently felt free to interpret the written constitution of the Western Region in a sense different from that of the majority.[20]

Why was the issue of the dismissal of a Premier by the Chief of State decided extra-legally and without recourse to Belgian constitutional practice in the Congo, but legally and in accordance with United Kingdom constitutional conventions in Nigeria? The answer may simply lie in the fact that the first two Congolese lawyers received their degrees from the University of Lovanium in Léopoldville in 1961—[21] after the "solution" of the constitutional crisis by the tragic death of Patrice Lumumba. In Nigeria, however, there was no dearth of qualified counsel, at least outside the Northern Region.[22]

But in all probability, the answer lies somewhere else: in the magic attraction of the British constitutional model for nations new and old,[23] and in Commonwealth

---

[19] Nigeria (Constitution) Order in Council, 1960, Fourth Schedule, STAT. INSTR., 1960, No. 1652.

[20] Akintola v. Governor of Western Nigeria and Adegbenro (FSC 187/1962). The full text of this decision was not available to the Editor; the above description relies on the report of Davies, *Nigeria—Some Recent Decisions on the Constitution*, 11 INT'L & COMP. L. Q. 919, 919-20, 924-25, and 933-35 (1962).

[21] See Report, *République du Congo (Léopoldville)*, in Symposium, "African Legal Education," 6 J. AFRICAN LAW 75, 92 (1962). On legal education in Africa, see also Paul, *Legal Education in English-Speaking Africa*, 15 J. LEGAL ED. 189 (1962). "Phineas Phogmore," *Aboriginal Legal Education in East Africa*, 14 *id.* 353 (1962) deals with quite a different subject. It is, to a surprising extent, a satirical parallel to our plea not to seek too much "uniqueness" in African legal systems.

[22] See Ademola, *Personnel Problems in the Administration of Justice in Nigeria, infra* p. 576, at 580.

[23] Especially constitution-makers outside of the Commonwealth might well heed the warning of Needler, *On the Dangers of Copying from the British*, 57 POL. SCI. Q. 379 (1962).

solidarity of constitutional conventions in the relationship between Governors-General (or Governors) and Premiers.[24] Such a solidarity seems understandable, but still a bit strange to observers from the United States. Here, we turn to our last point of inquiry. Why, it may be asked, has the United States contributed so little to the constitutional law of the new African states, even the Anglophonic ones? For as judged by the four standard criteria for differentiation between the United States and the British constitutions (a written instrument, federalism, judicial review, ministerial responsibility), the new African states such as Nigeria follow the United States three times out of four.

One explanation—certainly not to be discounted—may be the predominantly British (*i.e.*, almost invariably English) training of the senior members of the bar in Anglophonic African states. Another theory is a bit more circuitous and vastly more flattering: the United States, the argument runs, influenced the B.N.A. Act and the Australian constitution as well as (together with these two) the Indian constitution. Consequently, it is contended, a constitution such as that of the Federation of Nigeria, while ostensibly relying on Indian, Canadian, and Australian models, is nevertheless basically shaped by United States constitutional concepts.

It is submitted that a third explanation—not claiming exclusive validity—is more weighty. United States constitutional law is neatly divided into two categories: (1) "litigious" constitutional law, *i.e.*, the outcome-determinative impact of the Constitution on a huge array of the legal controversies of individuals and corporations with and among each other, as well as their controversies with various governmental organs; and (2) institutional public law, *i.e.*, the structure, operation, and interaction of constitutional organs. Unfortunately, only the former, which is of relatively secondary interest to constitution-makers, is regularly taught at the law schools. And while there is probably no rival to United States political science in the methods of case study of political processes, a foreign statesman may well hesitate to turn to political scientists for counsel in the drafting of constitutional instruments.

* * * * *

The basic purpose of the above Foreword has been to suggest that African legal problems are mainly unique because of the frequency of atypical situations; that little danger to traditional "Western" values and concepts lurks in a specific "African" conception of law, national or international; and that finally, the really singular telescoping of articulate societal and legal development into an unprecedentedly short time span affords the comparative scholar a splendid opportunity not only to see other societies in actual development, but also to comprehend his own legal frame of reference more thoroughly—and more modestly.

HANS W. BAADE.

[24] See, *e.g.*, Franck, *The Governor General and the Head of State Functions*, 32 CAN. B. REV. 1084 (1954); EUGENE A. FORSEY, THE ROYAL POWER OF DISSOLUTION IN THE BRITISH COMMONWEALTH (1943); Campbell, *The Prerogative Power of Dissolution: Some Recent Tasmanian Precedents*, [1961] PUBLIC LAW 165.

AFRICAN LEGAL STUDIES—A SURVEY OF THE FIELD AND THE ROLE OF THE UNITED STATES

Denis V. Cowen[*]

Introduction

In the United States lawyers have been slow starters in the field of African studies. While American anthropologists and sociologists—and in more recent years, political scientists and economists—have been prolific in African research,[1] their legal colleagues have, with few exceptions,[2] remained silent. Perhaps this is attributable in some degree to the natural conservatism of the breed, or—as the less charitable may aver—to legal parochialism. More probably it is due to the pressing claims on time and money which are made in American law schools by less exotic and, it would seem, more immediately practical subjects; then, too, it must be borne in mind that the freedom of the United States from colonial commitments in Africa removed one of the incentives which induced lawyers in countries like Britain or France to devote themselves to this field. But perhaps the main reason for the late entry of American lawyers into this area is the fact that it is only in very recent years, with the upsurge of independence throughout Africa, that knowledge of African legal systems, and of their potential development, has become essential for the effective conduct of international relations and trade. The recently won freedom of African states has generated a new vitality, and has brought into focus new problems of world-wide importance.

But despite the comparative novelty in America of African legal studies, it would be a mistake to conclude that no work has been done in this field. While it is perhaps true that lawyers, as a class, have tended to be less prolific and, possibly, less influential in African studies than their colleagues in anthropology, sociology, political science, and history,[3] they have not in the past neglected African problems

---

[*] B.A. 1937, LL.B. 1939, LL.D. 1962, University of Cape Town, South Africa. Professor of Law and Director of the Center for Legal Research (New Nations), University of Chicago. Author of several books and articles on constitutional problems of the new nations, the latest being The Foundations of Freedom (1961).

[1] An impressive record of American achievement in these fields is to be found in Howard, *American Contributions to Social Science Research on Africa*, in U.S. Nat'l Comm'n for UNESCO, 8th National Conference, Africa and the United States—Images and Realities 111 (1961).

[2] Particularization in these matters is invidious.

[3] The contribution of anthropologists and sociologists in the field of African law and administration has, on the whole, been outstanding in quality and long-sustained. Colonel John Maclean, who had been appointed Chief Commissioner in British Kaffraria in 1852, published his *A Compendium of Kafir Laws and Customs* as far back as 1858. This consists of several valuable memoranda compiled, under Maclean's direction, by Messrs. Dugmore, Warner, Brownle, and Ayliff. Though not the work of professionally trained lawyers, Maclean's *Compendium* has long been regarded as an African legal classic. Extracts are to be found in Albert Kocourek & John Henry Wigmore (Eds.), Sources of Ancient and Primitive Law, reprinted in 1 The Evolution of Law Series 292-325 (1915). A great deal of the more recent legal writing by contemporary anthropologists and sociologists (for example, by Gluckman, Schapera, Bohannan, and many others) is indispensable to professional lawyers.

and institutions. On the contrary, pioneer work of the kind begun by an earlier generation of lawyers, like J. M. Sarbah and Casely Hayford in Ghana,[4] has been carried steadily forward, until today the corpus of legal literature in the African field is very considerable.[5]

But whatever the achievements of the past may have been, new and exciting opportunities in the African field are now being offered to lawyers, as new problems come clearly into focus. If it be true that law is, in large measure, a framework within which a community's social, political, and economic life has its being, it is only within comparatively recent years that in many parts of Africa the problem of adjusting and adapting the framework itself has become urgent, due, primarily, to the dramatic development since World War II of modern urban and industrial life, and their impact on tribal mores. And what is perhaps more important, it is only since the advent of their independence that the new nations themselves have, in modern times, had the full responsibility and opportunity to use law and legal institutions consciously as instruments in nation-building.

The growth of African nationalism and the upsurge of independence throughout the Continent have, indeed, given a powerful new fillip to the development of African studies; and in law, no less than in other fields, this marks the beginning of a new epoch. Much of what was achieved in Africa during the last century and the first half of the twentieth century was achieved within a colonial context, and within the limits set by colonial policy. The possibilities and perspectives are now vastly different. A great opportunity is at hand for lawyers in Africa to do a major job of social engineering, such as Roscoe Pound advocated in the United States fifty years ago.

It would, of course, be egregiously naïve to assume that African legal development began in the colonial era. Long before European colonization, Africans had made their own contribution to law and its administration;[6] and now they are free to do so again. But on this occasion the challenge is greater than ever before. For the first time African states are taking their place as adult members of an international society; and within their own borders, they are beginning to grapple with the formidable task of welding together what was good in the colonial heritage,

[4] J. M. SARBAH, FANTI CUSTOMARY LAWS (1st ed. 1897; 2d ed. 1904), and FANTI NATIONAL CONSTITUTION (1906); CASELY HAYFORD, GOLD COAST NATIVE INSTITUTIONS (1903).

[5] Here again, particularization is invidious, and a comprehensive bibliography is beyond the scope of this paper. Suffice it to say that the volume of authoritative writing by lawyers in African countries has in recent years grown enormously, especially in Nigeria (e.g., Elias, Coker, and Ajayi), Ghana (e.g., Branford Griffith, Redwar, Rattray, Danquah, and Ollennu), French-speaking West Africa (d'Arboussier), and South Africa; and that no bibliography of African studies would be adequate which did not take account of the contributions made, among English lawyers, by Professors Arthur Phillips and J. N. D. Anderson and Dr. A. N. Allott; among French lawyers, by Luchaire, Rolland, and Lampue; among Belgian lawyers, by Sohier and Solus; and among Dutch lawyers, by Kollewijn and Korn.

Valuable bibliographies are to be found in A. ARTHUR SCHILLER, SYLLABUS IN AFRICAN LAW (1961); P. J. IDENBURG (ED.), THE FUTURE OF CUSTOMARY LAW IN AFRICA (1956); T. O. ELIAS, THE NATURE OF AFRICAN CUSTOMARY LAW (1956); A. N. ALLOTT, ESSAYS IN AFRICAN LAW (1960); and in the various issues of the *Journal of African Law* (vols. 1-5, 1957-1961), edited by Dr. A. N. Allott.

[6] See *infra* note 67 and accompanying text.

and indeed what they may find to be good anywhere, with what they deem worthy of preservation in their own indigenous institutions—so as to make a stable, healthy, and viable whole.

And so, it is perhaps worthwhile, as new vistas begin to open up, to take stock of the position and give some attention to the *why*, the *what*, and the *how* of legal work in this field.

A. Identifying the Legal Problem Areas in Africa

A comprehensive and systematic discussion of the subject matter of this study, even if confined to basic aspects, would require a treatise, rather than a single paper, and—more pertinently—it would call for range of knowledge, experience, and interest beyond the scope of most men, and certainly beyond mine.

A start may be made, however, by attempting to formulate some of the main legal problems that await solution in contemporary Africa; or, more accurately and also more modestly, one may begin by outlining the legal "problem areas." And thereafter it may be helpful to discuss what can and should be done to help—both in Africa itself, and outside Africa.

Looking at the matter from the inside, so to speak, from within Africa itself, it is fair to say that the subjects within the lawyer's province which are likely to hold the main interest of Africans throughout the continent for a substantial period of time—and which, I believe, should also hold the interest of American scholars—fall broadly under six heads. These may be specified briefly and in summary form as follows, reserving fuller explanation and discussion for later in this paper:

1. *The phenomenon of cultural and legal pluralism,* with particular reference to the nature and future of indigenous "customary law" and of other "personal" systems in Africa.
2. *The problems to which cultural and legal pluralism gives rise,* with particular reference to the evolution of national legal systems and their role in nation-building; the problem of interpersonal or internal conflict of laws; and the mutual interaction and accommodation of Romanistic and English common law systems within a single political unit.
3. *The reform of private law,* with particular reference to the accommodation in African legal systems of the facts of growing industrialization and urbanization; the development and improvement of the law relating to land-tenure, succession, the family, and the status of women; and with particular reference, also, to the provision of an adequate corpus of modern commercial and industrial law.
4. *Constitutional and administrative law,* with special reference to the technique of constitution-making; the adaptation of various forms of government—both foreign and indigenous—to accommodate local and contemporary needs; the status and future of chiefs; the status and organization of the Courts and the legal profession;

"the rule of law" and the protection of civil liberties; and the control of administrative agencies, especially in the light of the growth of state-controlled economic enterprises.

5. *International law and legal studies,* conceived in a broad context of international relations and organization; international banking, trade and investment; the amelioration of economic underdevelopment; and the relevance and future role in Africa of the European Common Market and of African organizations of a similar kind.

6. *Legal education,* with special reference to the role of comparative law and legal history; the teaching of the elements of Romanistic legal systems to students with a British or American background; the problem of interpreting the United States legal system in an English common law setting, and *vice versa.*

There are no doubt those who would prefer to group these topics under other, perhaps more suggestive and fruitful headings. Again, it is probable that there are important topics which have been omitted from this brief summary but which claim and will receive attention. Moreover, it must be borne in mind that emphases and priorities will vary from time to time in different parts of Africa. The priorities, for example, in Nigeria are not the same as those in the Cameroons or in Ethiopia, and these differ in turn from the priorities in, say, South Africa or in the Central African Federation. Differences of opinion on these matters do, in fact, exist and they are healthy; for they serve to focus attention on the old Aristotelian truth that at the beginning of any subject lies the problem of asking the right questions, and they may also induce a decent humility in any attempt to define the scope of African legal studies.

But, broadly speaking, it may, I think, be accepted that the "problem areas" enumerated above are, and will for some time remain, of compelling interest to the African continent as a whole. This may become more readily apparent when, presently, I deal more fully with each in turn.

B. *Differences in the Potential Interest of Various Countries and Institutions, and in Their Capacity to Contribute*

When we look to the contribution which various countries may have to make towards the solution of African problems, it appears helpful to draw certain distinctions.

In the first place it should be emphasized that there are aspects of African legal studies which have jurisprudential interest of a more or less universal character. Among these may be cited the problems of "reception," "infiltration," and "hybridization," and the respective roles of legislation, custom, the judicial process and professional opinion in legal development.[7] In these fields familiarity with some African material may do much to stimulate jurisprudential studies in any major law

[7] In regard to one specific but important aspect of the role of legislation, see *infra* at 552-53.

school anywhere.[8] It adds materially to the interest of a course on the nature of the legal process in modern Western societies to call attention to differences in approach and emphasis obtaining in other societies in regard to such matters as, for example, the role of the judge or the legal practitioner in litigation or arbitration; and it is plainly valuable to try to account for the differences. Nor is there any longer much excuse for neglecting these and similar topics; for a substantial and relevant body of literature has begun to accumulate, especially in recent years, in regard to Africa.[9]

On the other hand there are many subjects of less universal and more localized interest, in regard to which it is by no means the case that all countries are equipped to make an effective contribution or, indeed, would be interested in trying to do so. Thus, to cite an example given by Professor Max Rheinstein,[10] differences in school background, methods of instruction and examination, and—above all—in the length of time required to obtain a professional qualification, will no doubt continue to induce Africans from former British territories to study at British institutions of legal education rather than at American universities—at any rate at the first degree level. And in those parts of Africa where the legal system is Romanistic, it need hardly be said the basic legal training will continue to take place either in Africa or in Europe.

At the postgraduate level, however, the scope for African legal studies is plainly wider, though here again, the range of available facilities and probable specialization will differ from country to country, and indeed from university to university. It would, for example, seem quite natural for, say, a Canadian university to give particular attention to problems of legal pluralism, federalism, and closer association in West Africa, taking in both the areas which were formerly under British control and the French-speaking areas. Indeed certain Canadian universities may be in a peculiarly favorable position in this regard, not only because of language facilities, but also because of the psychological advantage which may derive from previous non-commitment in the colonial field.

In Africa itself interesting possibilities of potential specialization present themselves. South African and Rhodesian universities, for example, are potentially well placed to study and aid the growth of a legal system which aims not only at accommodating indigenous African and Islamic elements with non-indigenous (Western)

[8] Compare Dr. A. L. Goodhart's foreword to MAX GLUCKMAN, THE JUDICIAL PROCESS AMONG THE BAROTSE OF NORTHERN RHODESIA (1955), and Dean Roscoe Pound's foreword to HUNTINGTON CAIRNS, LAW AND THE SOCIAL SCIENCES (1935).

[9] See, for example, ARNOLD L. EPSTEIN, JUDICIAL TECHNIQUES AND THE JUDICIAL PROCESS: A STUDY IN AFRICAN CUSTOMARY LAW (1954); MAX GLUCKMAN, THE JUDICIAL PROCESS AMONG THE BAROTSE OF NORTHERN RHODESIA (1955); T. O. ELIAS, THE NATURE OF AFRICAN CUSTOMARY LAW (1956); ARTHUR PHILLIPS, NATIVE TRIBUNALS IN KENYA (1948); PAUL BOHANNAN, JUSTICE AND JUDGMENT AMONG THE TIV (1957); Hoebel, *Three Studies in African Law,* 13 STAN. L. REV. 418 (1961). *Cf.* KARL N. LLEWELLYN & E. ADAMSON HOEBEL, THE CHEYENNE WAY (1941); E. ADAMSON HOEBEL, THE POLITICAL ORGANIZATION AND LAW-WAYS OF THE COMANCHE INDIANS (1940).

[10] UNIVERSITY OF CHICAGO LAW SCHOOL, HIGHER EDUCATION, LAW AND TRAINING FOR THE LAW IN AFRICA (mimeo. 1961).

elements, but which may also achieve a fusion of Romanistic and Anglo-American legal thought. For the time being this exciting role may be played more actively in West Africa than in South Africa; but one day, when present racial preoccupations, stupidities, and digressions have passed away,[11] Southern Africa will, hopefully, contribute in full and great measure to a rich and distinctively African legal development.

Again, an undoubted need would be met by the early establishment in various parts of Africa of centers or institutes for comparative legal research of an advanced nature. That difficulties stand in the way of an undertaking of this kind is clear. There are, for example, delicate questions concerning location, and the relationship, if any, between such institutes and governments and other centers of higher learning. But these problems are not insuperable—as, for instance, the experience of the Indian Law Institute or (to give a different example) the Institute for Advanced Legal Studies (London) has shown; and the sooner they are grappled with in an African context the better for the future of African legal studies and indeed the future of Africa itself.

Such being the range of this subject, it is necessary to put on one side any pretensions to comprehensiveness, and to try to limit the field to what one may hope to manage in a single paper. To this end I shall try to elucidate the "problem areas" of contemporary Africa as effectively as I can, but in regard to what can and should be done in various countries to help in the "solution" of problems, or and should be done in various countries to help in the "solution" of problems, or to advance research, I shall confine myself to what I think might usefully be attempted by American legal scholars.

I

The Problem Areas

A. The Phenomenon of Cultural and Legal Pluralism

Basic to an understanding of contemporary Africa is the phenomenon of cultural and legal pluralism—that is to say, the present fact (whatever the future may hold) that in most parts of Africa peoples of different ethnic, cultural, and religious groups live within one and the same political unit under different systems of law.

To begin with, in most territories several different varieties of "customary," or indigenous, African law operate side by side. Matrilineal systems, for example, differ significantly from patrilineal ones; and within each of these systems, in turn, there are tribal and regional variations.

Then, too, account must be taken of the fundamental role that has been played in the past in various regions of Africa, and which is still being played, by particular Western legal systems, such as the English common law, French law, Roman-Dutch

---

[11] There is a tendency among some scholars, and not a few institutions and foundations, to "write off" South Africa as hopeless or too hot to handle. This is both short-sighted and unnecessarily timorous. It is unsound to equate South Africa, her peoples—black, white, and brown—and her universities with the policies of any particular government or even sequence of governments.

law, and the laws of Belgium, Portugal, and Spain. These laws—the laws of colonizing or former colonizing powers—have in the past all played well-defined roles which bear re-examination. Each has, moreover, imprinted its distinctive character on many aspects of national life; and though the future of these laws may be somewhat more difficult to assess, it is unlikely that their influence will be obliterated. Nor—unless I much mistake the climate of opinion—would Africans wish this influence to be obliterated, for although the application of these Western legal systems may sometimes in the past have been confided to fallible, because human, hands, both the systems themselves—and, let it be added, their practitioners—have made great contributions. The entire eradication of the colonial legal system, even were it desired, would leave large and ragged gaps.

In this picture of legal and cultural pluralism, an added complication—or, as I prefer to say, a source of enrichment—arises in those areas where Islamic and Hindu groups are strong and where account must be taken of their laws.

However, to state the phenomenon of cultural and legal pluralism in this summary fashion is to give it a misleading clarity. It is one thing, for example, to say that various systems of "customary law" operate in Africa; it is quite another to ascertain with precision what rules these systems prescribe, and what are the similarities and differences between the systems themselves.[12] Precise groundwork of this kind is difficult and laborious, but essential. It is essential because where, as is often the case, it is sought to change or to build upon a customary institution, one should know exactly what one is dealing with. It is difficult work because—to mention two points only—customary law often lacks, or defies circumscription within, a formal or conceptual framework, and, further, what is called "customary law" in Africa is often in the process of rapid change—changing, in fact, while the work of recording goes on. Fortunately this work is now being undertaken, on a broad scale, under the able direction of Dr. A. N. Allott at the School of Oriental and African Studies in London.

In this regard, the compilation of comprehensive bibliographies should be regarded as complementary and equally essential groundwork. Masses of valuable legal material lie buried in rare and out-of-print "blue-books" and other official publications; and often, too, they are be found, like flies in amber, in unexpected places—in the pages of journals which lawyers seldom read. Years of work lie ahead in making the currently existing material more generally known and readily available;[13] and it is to be hoped that in this task the unusually rich resources of the South African and Rhodesian archives will not be neglected.

Again, it is one thing to say that peoples of various groups live in Africa under different laws, but this leaves out of account the fact, which anthropologists have stressed in recent years, that the line of demarcation between the groups is often

---

[12] See generally, A. N. ALLOTT, *The Unity of African Law*, in ESSAYS IN AFRICAN LAW 55-71 (1960).

[13] Here, Dr. A. N. Allott of the School of Oriental and African Studies, University of London, and Professor A. Arthur Schiller of Columbia University, are to be congratulated on making a start with the compilation of accurate and scholarly bibliographies.

for from clear-cut. Especially in African urban communities, it is becoming increasingly blurred.

All this is not to deny that cultural and legal pluralism is still a basic fact in contemporary Africa. It does, however, call attention, at the very outset of African legal studies, to the need to examine the actual phenomenon itself, that is to say, its more precise details as well as its broad outlines, its future trends as well as its existing contours.

B. The Problems to Which Cultural and Legal Pluralism Gives Rise

Cultural and legal pluralism is, of course, by no means new, nor does the continent of Africa have any monopoly of it and of the problems to which it gives rise. Every student of legal history is familiar with the broad outlines of this phenomenon during what may be regarded as its heyday in Europe, from the decline of the Roman Empire until the rise of the principle of territoriality in the eleventh and twelfth centuries A.D.[14] And, no doubt, equally familiar are the contemporary examples in the Middle East and in Indonesia.

Though the problems to which cultural and legal pluralism gives rise are manifold, there are among them at least three of major interest in contemporary Africa; and each will severely tax the lawyer's skill and the politician's wisdom.

The first and most fundamental problem may, perhaps, be stated as follows: to what extent should the condition of cultural and legal pluralism be allowed to continue? More specifically, if legal pluralism is severable from cultural pluralism, to what extent should legal pluralism be discouraged? That cultural pluralism may continue as a fact, for some time, is plain. But in several African states today there is a discernible tendency to foster the development of a single national legal system, and to play down the role of laws which are personal to religious, tribal, and ethnic groups. Various reasons may be given for this trend, but perhaps the most obvious ones are that a uniform national legal system may aid the development of national unity and sentiment, and, if conceived on modern lines, may at the same time contribute towards the "modernization" of a country previously regarded as "backward." It was partly for these reasons that in Turkey in 1926 Kemal Atatürk sought to eliminate pluralism at one stroke by the radical substitution of a modern law of Swiss origin for the then prevailing multiplicity of personal religious laws in the Ottoman Empire.[15]

Now, although in contemporary Africa the facts of urbanization and industrialization have already wrought big changes in customary law and sapped its strength, it remains true that there are obvious dangers in attempting to force the pace along the lines favored by Kemal Atatürk. Not only may such an attempt prove divisive

---

[14] The leading work in the field is probably still KARL NEUMEYER, DIE GEMEINRECHTLICHE ENTWICKLUNG DES INTERNATIONALEN PRIVAT—UND STRAFRECHTS BIS BARTOLUS (2 vols.) (1901 and 1906).

[15] See, generally, *Le Colloque d'Istanbul sur le Problème de la Réception des droits étrangers*, 6 ANNALES DE LA FACULTÉ DE DROIT D'ISTANBUL v-xii, 1-251 (1956).

rather than unifying, but it would seem that there are other more thorough-going and effective methods of encouraging the growth of a uniform legal system.

Some branches of law are more deeply and emotionally involved with the life and culture of a people than others and hence more resistant to sudden and radical change by legislative fiat. This is the case, for example, with family law and the law of succession as distinct from, say, the law relating to such impersonal transactions as negotiable instruments. For this reason, family law may well lend itself more easily, and ultimately, more effectively, to adaptation and development by the gradual process of judicial interpretation and the influence of professional opinion, rather than by radical legislative reform.[16] However, even within the field of family law, generalizations of this kind should, in the present state of knowledge, be made with caution. It is, for example, being suggested in Ghana at the present time that polygamy may be discouraged by a statutory provision to the effect that only one "marriage" may be registered, and that only the spouse of a registered union shall be entitled to succeed on intestacy.[17] The effect of the proposal, if it becomes law, and of the indirect sanction which it imposes, will be studied with interest. Another fruitful approach to the general problem, although limited in scope, would seem to be that favored by the late Hans Cory in Tanganyika, that is to say, the study at depth of a group of related (for example, matrilineal) customary systems, with a view to their recordation and gradual unification after full discussion with tribal elders.[18]

But whatever the course of wisdom may be in a particular case, or in regard to particular branches of law, the essential point to stress for present purposes is that the nationalization or "modernization" of legal systems and the eradication of pluralism, even where desirable, are delicate tasks that call for a high order of statesmanship, as well as considerable legal skill and knowledge, especially of a comparative and historical kind. It is partly for this reason that an early start in the comparative study of law and legal techniques should be encouraged in the currently developing African law schools. It would, for example, be very shortsighted for African governments and their advisers to ignore the lessons which countries like India, Turkey, and Japan have to offer in the process of developing and modernizing their legal systems.

Moreover, there should be added to the techniques of significant comparative study the illumination to be gained from legal history. Problems concerning the interaction of various legal systems, problems of "hybridization" and "infiltration"— now looming large in contemporary Africa[19]—are, indeed, the very staple of legal history; and they merit a place in any realistically planned African law curriculum

---

[16] Compare the conclusions reached by the London Conference, in THE LONDON CONFERENCE ON THE FUTURE OF LAW IN AFRICA, RECORD OF PROCEEDINGS (Allott ed. 1960). See 4 J. AFRICAN LAW 1 (1960). And see JAMES BRYCE, *Roman Law and English Law*, in 1 STUDIES IN HISTORY AND JURISPRUDENCE 98, 124 *et seq.* (1901).
[17] The Marriage, Divorce, and Succession bill of 1962, introduced by the Minister of Justice.
[18] HANS CORY, SEKUMA LAW AND CUSTOM (1953).
[19] See generally Twining, *Some Aspects of Reception*, 5 SUDAN L. J. AND REPORTS 229 (1960).

that purports to offer more than a severely practical vocational training. I do not, of course, underestimate the urgent need for practical "bread and butter" lawyers in contemporary Africa, but wish merely to emphasize that Africa demands, and deserves, more in addition.

A second great complex of problems to which legal pluralism gives rise is that which has generally come to be known under the heading of inter-personal conflict of laws, internal conflict of laws, or inter-gentile law (inter-gentiel recht).[20] How should one regulate disputes between members of different ethnic or religious groups living within the same political unit under different laws—for example, between a Yoruba and a Hausa in Nigeria, between a Zulu and a Xhosa in South Africa, or between a white settler and a Swazi in Swaziland?

African colonizing powers have approached this problem in various ways, which may, however, conveniently be grouped under two heads: (i) the approach in territories which are or have been under British or white South African influence; (ii) the approach in territories which are or have been under continental (*e.g.*, French or Belgian) influence. Within each group significant variations occur from territory to territory. For example, French and Belgian practice are distinguishable, as are Kenyan, Nigerian, and South African practice.[21] But, for the purposes of the broad survey here being attempted, it is necessary to pass by the finer distinctions.

In territories which are or have been under British or white South African influence it is usual to distinguish between

(a) inter-personal conflicts concerning transactions entered into between members of the white colonizing group, on the one hand, and members of the indigenous African or other groups, on the other hand; and

(b) inter-personal conflicts in disputes which do not involve members of the white colonizing group.

In addition, one finds in these territories a dual and sometimes a multiple set of courts: "Native Courts" for disputes between the indigenous Africans; another set of courts—variously designated as Magistrates' Courts, Superior and High Courts—for litigation between white persons or between whites and others; and in places where, for example, Islamic influence is strong, Sharia Courts for the adherents of Islam.

In the territories which we are now discussing, both the law imported by the colonizing power, and the higher courts established by it, have hitherto enjoyed a special and superior status. To begin with, the law of the colonizing power performs a two-fold function. First, it serves in large measure as an overriding common law

---

[20] Various terminologies have been suggested: see Schiller, Book Review, 4 J. AFRICAN LAW 175 (1960). See generally, R. D. KOLLEWIJN, INTERGENTIEL RECHT (1955).

[21] For a lucid introductory sketch, see ARTHUR PHILLIPS, *Recognition and Application of Native Law*, in SURVEY OF AFRICAN MARRIAGE AND FAMILY LIFE 176-89 (1953). That South African practice is more color-conscious than practice in most British colonies is plain, but it is equally plain that a color line has operated in these matters in British colonies generally.

for the entire territory, applicable to all persons whatever their ethnic or religious group may be, especially in cases of serious crime.[22] Similarly, where in the view of the colonizing power, African law and custom is repugnant to natural justice and sound morality, cases may be decided in accordance with "natural justice," which in practice tends to be what is prescribed by the law of the colonizing power.[23]

Secondly, the law of the colonizing power serves as the white man's own tribal law—a tribal law, however, of special status; for whereas Africans are compulsorily subject to certain branches of the colonizer's law, whites are not subject to any branch of African customary law to which they have not expressly or impliedly submitted themselves.

The assumption of superiority becomes even more apparent when one examines the jurisdiction of the courts. The general pattern is that whereas the jurisdiction of "Native Courts" is limited both as to subject matter and persons (they ordinarily have no jurisdiction over white persons who have not consented to their jurisdiciton),[24] the courts possessing jurisdiction over whites not only enjoy much more extensive original and appellate jurisdiction (in the upper hierarchy, full jurisdiction), but also have supervisory and appellate jurisdiction over the "Native Courts."

The system outlined above has shortcomings. Not only does it perpetuate racial divisions in a hard and fast way, but it also not infrequently leads to anomalous and unjust results, especially in cases where Africans are denied the benefits, as distinct from the burdens, of the colonizing power's law.

The nature of these anomalies may, perhaps, be illustrated by a few South African cases. Whatever the technical justification may be, it is not easy to explain to the satisfaction of a fair-minded person why a man married according to African law and custom should be held liable for household necessaries purchased by his "wife,"[25] but that when it comes to the privileges accorded to husband and wife by the law of evidence, a person married according to African law and custom is in the same position as an unmarried person.[26] Nor is it easy to explain why a white widow, who had married under Roman-Dutch common law, is entitled (despite contributory negligence on her husband's part) to damages against a person who negligently caused her husband's death, whereas an African widow, who had married under customary law, is denied a similar remedy where her husband's death is negligently caused by a white man.[27]

---

[22] For critical comment, see Holleman, *The Recognition of Bantu Customary Law in South Africa*, in P. J. IDENBURG (ED.), THE FUTURE OF CUSTOMARY LAW IN AFRICA 233 (1956).

[23] Practices varies from territory to territory.

[24] The extent to which whites may consent to the jurisdiction of "Native Courts" differs from territory to territory.

[25] Zondani v. Maaske, 18 E.D.C. 71.

[26] An Act to Consolidate the Laws Relating to Procedure and Evidence in Criminal Proceedings and Matters Incidental Thereto, Act No. 56 of 1955, § 226(3) (So. Africa).

[27] Mokwena v. Laub, [1943] W.L.D. 63. There are some startling statements in the judgment: ". . . native customs are not applicable to civilized people. . . . there is no suggestion that this legality is anything more than the legality which arises under native law and custom, and the defendant being a European, is not bound by legality of that kind." *Id.* at 67.

The pattern adopted in territories colonized by European continental powers has several distinctive features of its own. While it would be extravagant to suggest that continental European colonizers are innocent of the notion that the colonizer's law has inherent superiority, it would seem that the continental approach has avoided some of the defects which have manifested themselves in other regimes. The key idea is that by satisfying certain *"conditions d'assimilation,"* that is to say, upon attaining a defined level of "civilization," an African might entirely change his legal status. For example, by being registered as an "immatriculated native" in the Congo, an African ceased to live under tribal law and became subject to localized Belgian law.[28]

By allowing Africans to move more or less freely from one status to another, the continental approach has, in part, avoided the dangers of administering justice on racial lines.[29] But when this has been said, it must be owned that the whole subject of inter-personal conflict of laws is in need of reform throughout Africa. Significant reforms have already been effected in Ghana since Independence,[30] but the over-all task will be a long and delicate one. Here again, however, I would suggest that much of value may be contributed by the techniques of comparative law and the illumination of legal history. Let me now briefly state what I have in mind.

Many years ago, in explaining the rationale of the subject of conflict of laws, Dicey pointed out that there were a limited number of courses theoretically open to a court when faced with a conflicts problem.[31] In the first place, it might refuse to entertain the suit. Secondly, it might assume jurisdiction in an appropriate case, but apply exclusively the substantive rules of the *lex fori* in determining the rights of the parties. Thirdly, it might assume jurisdiction, and directly determine the rights of the parties in accordance with a specially developed body of substantive law—a kind of *jus gentium* or *lex communis*—which would be neither the *lex fori* nor any one of the conflicting systems involved in the litigation. And, finally, the court might assume jurisdiction in accordance with certain rules, and then apply rules of conflict of laws in the strict sense, that is to say, rules which do not directly determine the rights of the parties, but which point to the legal system best suited in the particular case to do so.

Each of these possibilities has well-authenticated historical precedents. Thus, the first was once the attitude adopted by the English courts;[32] the second was the trend

[28] For a brief summary in English, with reference also to French and Portuguese practice, see ARTHUR PHILLIPS, SURVEY OF AFRICAN MARRIAGE AND FAMILY LIFE 181 *et seq.* (1953).

[29] It would, however, be a mistake to exaggerate its merits. Before 1948, the process of "immatriculation" in the Congo was simple and in several cases automatic; thereafter it became a more arduous and discretionary procedure, and the standard for admission to the status of immatriculation became that of "middle-class respectability in a typical Belgian city"—a phrase used by Dr. Phillip Whittaker, of Makere, at a seminar held in the Law School, University of Chicago.

[30] See, especially, the Courts Law of 21st June, 1960.

[31] A. V. DICEY, A DIGEST OF THE LAW OF ENGLAND WITH RESPECT TO THE CONFLICT OF LAWS (1st ed. 1896).

[32] Sack, *Conflicts of Laws in the History of the English Law,* in 3 LAW: A CENTURY OF PROGRESS, 1835-1935, at 342, 344 (1937).

of English decisions during the eighteenth century, and, in modern times, it has, in various forms, again found champions—notably in the United States;[33] the third was, in part, favored by the Romans; while the fourth is what may be called the currently orthodox approach of conflict of laws.

Putting the first possibility aside because, if uniformly adopted, it would result everywhere in a complete denial of justice, African communities have an opportunity, in this formative stage of their jurisprudence, to re-examine each of the three other alternatives, to look again at the foundations of the conflict of laws, and adapt to their own purposes what best suits their needs.

This is not the occasion to examine the possibilities of adaptation in detail. But it may be of some use to venture a few broad generalizations. In the first place, the exclusive application of the *lex lori* would often defeat the reasonable expectations of the parties, unless the rules of jurisdiction were elaborated so extensively as to embrace virtually all of what is now called "choice of law"—an objection stated by Dicey sixty-five years ago and, specifically, by the seventeenth century Dutch statutists. Moreover, this objection would appear to hold good whether one exclusively applies the *lex fori* to conflicts between territorial legal systems, or intra-territorially to inter-personal conflicts adjudicated upon by dual sets of courts administering different "personal" legal systems.

The Roman idea of developing a *lex communis* or modern *jus gentium* may have more to offer in contemporary Africa—at any rate for intra-territorial disputes between members of various groups engaging in transactions of a particular kind. Increasingly, for example, there is a tendency especially in urban areas in several African states—and it would seem to be a healthy tendency—for certain transactions to be governed by a new body of law, a uniformly applicable *jus gentium,* which is neither traditional customary law nor Western imported law.[34]

On the other hand, the same technique may not be suited to all cases. Indeed, in these matters, it would seem that African lawyers would be well advised to remain discriminatingly eclectic; and for some problems a more fruitful approach may be that of orthodox conflict of laws, which, of course, presupposes the existence and applicability of separate non-uniform laws.

In speaking of the approach of what has here been called "orthodox conflict of laws," it is important to remember that most of its current doctrines were evolved in a comparatively few centuries subsequent to the age of the Glossators. Again, most of its principles were developed within an international context of "territorial" legal systems, that is to say, systems in which a single body of law is generally and *prima facie* applicable to all persons within a given territory. Plainly these principles

---

[33] This appears to be the trend of thought of Professor Albert Ehrenzweig in his recent and valuable treatise, CONFLICT OF LAWS (1962). Professor Brainerd Currie of Duke University, while favoring the application of the policy of the *lex fori* in the event of a genuine conflict, emphasizes the importance of giving substantive rather than formal definition to what is a conflict case. His stimulating essays are being published in collected form by the Duke University Press.

[34] Compare ARTHUR PHILLIPS, SURVEY OF AFRICAN MARRIAGE AND FAMILY LIFE 186 (1953).

have a role to play in conflict cases arising as between different territorial legal units in Africa (*Rechtsgebiete* or *territoria juris*); and it would seem, too, that they may have an analogical use in solving the kind of problem with which we are at present concerned, namely, intra-territorial conflicts of an inter-personal kind.

There is, however, another chapter in the early history of private international law which may also have a contribution to offer towards the solution of our problem, at any rate for the period during which legal pluralism remains, an actual fact, which in some territories may be a long period. I refer to those centuries in Europe after the fall of Rome but before the rise of the modern principle of territoriality, during which there operated the so-called regime of personal laws.

In a famous passage quoted by Savigny, Agobard (Archbishop of Lyons) tells us how during the regime of personal laws it often happened "that five men, each living under a different law, might be found walking or sitting together."[35] The Visigoth, the Frank, the Burgundian, the Lombard, the Frisian, and so on, each lived under his own personal law.

It is usual nowadays for some writers on conflict of laws to make a polite but perfunctory bow to this branch of learning in a few paragraphs of elegant diversion under some such title as Historical Antecedents. It is also usual to discount the subject as being of mere antiquarian interest.[36] This, I submit, is a pity; for when the subject is studied more closely, and the operative rules examined, it becomes clear that in those early centuries a more flexible and sophisticated method of solving inter-personal conflicts was practiced than at present obtains in many African territories—more flexible, for example, than the following rule of thumb which obtains in South Africa:[37]

In any suit or proceedings between Natives who do not belong to the same tribe, the Court shall not, in the absence of any agreement between them with regard to the particular system of Native law to be applied in such suit or proceedings, apply any system of Native law other than that which is in operation at the place where the defendant or respondent resides or carries on business or is employed, or if two or more different systems are in operation at that place, not being within a tribal area, the Court shall not apply any such system unless it is the law of the tribe (if any), to which the defendant or respondent belongs.

At the turn of the last century scholars like Neumeyer in Germany,[38] Stouff in France[39] and Catellani in Italy[40] did pioneer work in bringing to light the broad outlines and rationale of the rules which were applied during the era of personal laws; and much has been added to our knowledge of that period in recent years.

[35] "Es geschieht oft, dass fünf Menschen zusammen gehen oder sitzen, von welchen jeder nach einem andern Recht lebt." 1 Friedrich Karl von Savigny, Geschichte des Römischen Rechts im Mittelalter 116 (1834).
[36] See, for example, Arthur Nussbaum, Principles of Private International Law 6-7 (1943).
[37] Native Administration Act, Act No. 38 of 1927, § 11(2) (So. Africa).
[38] Neumeyer, *op. cit. supra* note 14.
[39] *Étude sur le principle de la personalité des lois depuis les invasions barbares jusqu' au XIIe Siècle*, Revue Bourguignonne 1-65, 273-310 (1894).
[40] 1 Enrico L. Catellani, Diritto Internazionale Privato 197-265 (1895).

The opportunity is now at hand to put this knowledge to use in contemporary Africa, not, of course, by slavish copying, but by conscious adaptation of principles in so far as they may be found to be useful and acceptable.

The third and last aspect of legal pluralism to which I would here refer is the question of the inter-action between, and the mutual accommodation of, Romanistic and English common law systems in a single political unit. In their more poetic moments comparative lawyers are wont to talk about the fusion of two great streams of legal thought—Anglo-American and Romanistic. I like to think that this may be more than an idle dream, and that one of the chief areas of fusion will be contemporary Africa;[41] for it is perhaps not sufficiently realized how strong and widespread Romanistic legal elements are in Africa. The whole of Southern Africa, a major part of the Central African Federation, the Congo and the Portuguese territories, vast areas of West Africa, and parts of North Africa and Ethiopia—all have powerful infusions of Romanistic legal elements. And what is more to the point, there are several important areas in which English and Romanistic legal ideas are having to find a mutual *modus vivendi,* for example, in South Africa and in Southern Rhodesia where English ideas and an uncodified Romanistic system (Roman-Dutch law) have long co-existed and have tended either to fuse or complement each other. Interesting developments along similar lines may occur in the Cameroons, as between English law and a local codified French law, and, of course, in other parts of Africa, if Pan-African aspirations are fulfilled.

These considerations have a palpably close bearing on the subject of legal education, and especially on the role of comparative law, which will be discussed presently.

C. The Reform of Private Law

Passing on now to the subject of law reform, I shall be very brief. The priorities within the field of private law are reasonably clear: land-tenure, commercial and industrial transactions, marriage and succession. These are the subjects which increasingly claim the attention of the African law reformer.[42]

The traditional patterns of land tenure and land use in Africa are not wholly adequate to cope with the need for big increases in the production of food and other wealth by the use of modern agricultural and industrial methods. Nor, as it seems to many, do the old systems give adequate security of title in communities rapidly converting to a full-scale money economy. And, perhaps more important still, there exist few accurate statements in legally precise language of the old customary systems themselves. Inadequacy of rule in this important field is unfortunate enough, but uncertainty is intolerable. At the same time reform of land tenure is an exceptionally difficult and delicate task; for powerful interests are almost invariably involved, and the ramifications of change are often more far-

---

[41] If Britain joins the Common Market, Europe would, of course, be a focus of interest in this regard.
[42] See, generally, THE LONDON CONFERENCE ON THE FUTURE OF LAW IN AFRICA, RECORD OF THE PROCEEDINGS (Allott ed. 1960). See 4 J. AFRICAN LAW 1 (1960).

reaching than may appear at first sight. Years of arduous work lie ahead in this field.[43]

The claim to attention of modern commercial and industrial law is no less compelling, as is evident, for example, from the recent scholarly reports and practical work undertaken in Ghana on company legislation and the law of insolvency—work in which Professor L. C. B. Gower, of the London School of Economics, has played so distinguished a part.[44] Nor should the welding force of a uniform commercial code be lost from sight in those areas where experiments in closer political association and nation-building are now taking place.[45]

Again, in this time when economic and political changes are sweeping through Africa, family law, succession and the status of women must inevitably attract the attention of the law reformer. The increasingly important role which African women are playing in politics, the effect of urbanization, and the influence of religion are all leading to substantial modifications of the old mores.

D. Constitutional and Administrative Law

And now, having dealt at some length with topics of private law, it is time to pass on to the subject of constitutional and administrative law. The field is vast, so vast that it may seem almost an impertinence to attempt any kind of brief survey.[46] I propose, therefore, to pass rapidly and virtually without comment over many topics which, if space permitted, I would wish to deal with more adequately, both because of their importance and by reason of long sustained personal interest.

I can, for example, do no more here than mention as worthy of serious academic study and research in first-class law schools anywhere such subjects as the appropriateness and potential development of institutions of government when transplanted or grafted abroad;[47] the use that may be made of second chambers in a bicameral legislative system to accommodate a traditional chieftainship, or as one of the safeguards of a particular constitutional structure;[48] the relative merits of presidential and parliamentary "types" of executive government in contemporary Africa;

---

[43] There is a voluminous and ever-growing literature on the reform of land tenure. See, for example, A BIBLIOGRAPHY OF PUBLISHED SOURCES RELATING TO AFRICAN LAND TENURE (Colonial Office, London 1950); FOOD AND AGRICULTURE ORGANIZATION OF THE UNITED NATIONS, A BIBLIOGRAPHY OF LAND TENURE (1955); U.N. DEP'T OF ECONOMIC AFFAIRS, LAND REFORMS: DEFECTS IN AGRARIAN STRUCTURE AS OBSTACLES TO ECONOMIC DEVELOPMENT (ST/ECA/11) (U.N. Pub. Sales No. 1951.II.B.3.); REPORT OF THE WORKING PARTY ON AFRICAN LAND TENURE IN KENYA (1958).

[44] The relevant reports were published in Accra in 1961.

[45] As suggested by Professor Arthur Macmahon at the Symposium on Federalism in the New Nations, held under the auspices of the Center for Legal Research (New Nations), Chicago University Law School, in February, 1962: "It would be interesting to speculate what the history of the United States might have been had commercial law been a subject reserved to the federal legislature."

[46] For a short but valuable survey dealing with an important part of the field, see INT'L COMM'N OF JURISTS, AFRICAN CONFERENCE ON THE RULE OF LAW (1961).

[47] This is the subject of a study soon to be published by the Duke University Commonwealth Studies Center.

[48] A subject discussed at the Kenya Constitutional Conference held at Lancaster House, London, in February 1962, and of obvious interest in many other parts of Africa.

the potential role of hereditary Paramount Chiefs as Heads of State;[49] techniques of constitution-drafting and their suitability in particular situations—whether, for example, in drafting constitutional guarantees in African territories creative ambiguity is preferable to specific detail and definition; the advantages and disadvantages of the judicial review of legislation and governmental action by the ordinary courts or by special constitutional courts, and the various possible alternatives; the techniques and styles of constitutional interpretation; the meaning and significance of various conceptions of the separation of governmental powers; the drafting of criminal codes and penology, especially in areas where Islamic influence is strong, and so on.

These are matters some of which, no doubt, may best be dealt with in a university law school in collaboration with the department of government; but whatever the arrangement, they should not be ignored by lawyers, and especially not by those interested in African public law.

Now, while I must be content here with the bare enumeration of the above-mentioned topics, there are a few matters within the field of public law which I would like to discuss a little more specifically.

In the first place I think that it would be short-sighted for English-speaking law schools to concentrate on English and American ideas, admirable and relevant as they are, to the exclusion of all others in the study and exposition of constitutional, and especially administrative law. This practice, regrettably not infrequent, seems to derive in some quarters from a peculiar notion that all continental or Romanistically-based constitutional regimes are adverse to freedom.[50] Continental public law is, however, a storehouse of principle of considerable significance for contemporary Africa.

Consider, for example, ideas and practices like the modern continental alternatives to judicial review by the ordinary courts, or the German idea that, in the interests of freedom, legislation should apply generally[51]—especially legislative exceptions to constitutional guarantees—and that the need for protection should be focussed on administrative, rather than on legislative action. Not only are these ideas interesting in themselves, but they may well play an increasingly important role in Africa generally, by no means exclusively in areas where continental influence has in the past been strong.[52] If, as I believe, there is always a strong case for teaching constitutional and administrative law comparatively, it is especially strong in regard to contemporary Africa, which seems healthily determined to remain flexible in the pursuit of precedent and example.

[49] A subject of considerable current interest and technical complexity in Uganda, Barotseland, Basutoland, and Swaziland.

[50] It seems hardly necessary to point out that continental systems are not necessarily enmeshed in maxims like *quod principi placuit vigorem legis habet*.

[51] See, *e.g.*, article 19 of the Basic Law of the West German Republic.

[52] The influence of French ideas on the enforceability of constitutional guarantees has already made itself felt in the former British Cameroons; and the appointment of a Swiss constitutional lawyer to advise the KANU delegation at the recent Kenya Constitutional Conference (February 1962) is not without significance.

I turn now to more fundamental considerations which relate to what may be described as the challenge of contemporary Africa. Africa presents many challenges, two of which, however, are very relevant to our present subject. To begin with, there is a basic challenge to the Africans themselves; then there is an equally fundamental challenge which Africa presents to the rest of the world. I shall try to deal with each in turn.

The challenge to Africans is concerned very largely with the idea of freedom. Will the new African governments be equal to the challenge which freedom itself presents? Every African nationalist, in fact almost every articulate African, if asked what he means by freedom, in an African context, will tell you that part of the answer is that it means freedom from external control, freedom from colonialism. In other words, it means independence or self-determination—freedom to go one's own way, to learn by one's own efforts, and from one's own mistakes. When asked to pursue the analysis beyond mere freedom from external control, Africans usually, and very understandably, go on to include freedom from poverty, freedom from illiteracy and ignorance, freedom from ill-health, and freedom from the hardship and cruelty which exist when a society lacks a basic minimum of social security and social services.

And it is precisely at this point that Africa comes face to face with a fundamental challenge. The classic freedoms of the eighteenth and nineteenth centuries, among which the civil liberties and human rights enshrined in the United States Constitution and its amendments may be regarded as typical, all involve freedom from governmental action. They are in essence limitations upon what the state may legitimately do, statements of what governments may not do. But it has become increasingly clear in the twentieth century that there are essential services which the state not only can but also should undertake for its citizens. It is no longer sufficient to specify what may not be done; increasingly attention is being given to the state's positive duty to provide an environment in which the classic freedoms may be effectively enjoyed.[53]

Writing on this point some ten years ago, an Indian philosopher and poet, Humuyun Kabir, said.[54]

The problem of the twentieth century is to reconcile the conflicting claims of liberty and security. A new charter of human rights must secure to each individual, irrespective of race, color, sex or creed, the minimum requirements for human existence, namely, (a) the food and clothing necessary for maintaining the individual in health, (b) the housing necessary for protection against the weather and for allowing space for relaxation and enjoyment of leisure, (c) the education necessary for developing the latent faculties, and (d) the medical and sanitary services necessary for checking and curing disease and for insuring the health of the individual and the community.

[53] The point was emphasized at the Conference on the Rule of Law sponsored by the International Commission of Jurists at New Delhi in 1959. For a report on this Conference, see INT'L COMM'N OF JURISTS, THE RULE OF LAW IN A FREE SOCIETY (1960).
[54] Kabir, *Human Rights: The Islamic Tradition and the Problems of the World Today*, in HUMAN RIGHTS, COMMENTS AND INTERPRETATIONS—A SYMPOSIUM 191-94 (UNESCO, 1949).

Kabir is, no doubt, correct in seeing the problem as one of reconciling liberty and security. But how is this to be done; how is one to secure an adequate sufficiency of both interests?

The problem is difficult enough in the older countries of the West, which are already richly endowed with amenities, and where grinding poverty, illiteracy, and ill-health are, on the whole, more the exception than the rule. In these countries it is mainly the threat of global war which tends to arm the state with inflated power and threatens to erode both freedom and wealth. But in Africa today, for the majority of the people, hunger, illiteracy, and sickness are still a terrible scourge. Add to this the fact that communications and basic civic amenities remain rudimentary in vast areas of the continent, and take into account also the very understandable impatience of political leaders to effect a change, and the perennial problem of insuring human liberty takes on almost awesome proportions.

Democracy and human freedom will always have hard going where they are faced with grinding poverty, ill-health, and lack of education. The going will be even harder where, as is often the case in the new nations, it is sought to compress a century of gradual development into, say, ten years. And it is for this reason that many friends of Africa have asked sympathetically, but not without misgiving: can the independent African states take their place in the modern world as free democratic societies; can they provide the amenities and security which their people yearn for without resorting to dictatorship and the eradication of human freedom?

Faced with the evils referred to above, it is not surprising that some African politicians tend to attach more importance to the provision of security than to the safeguarding of individual liberty. Indeed, a few have become openly impatient with the whole idea of civil liberty and the restraints it places upon state action. For the time being, they say, the classic nineteenth century freedoms, however desirable in themselves, may, alas, have to remain for them and their people a luxury which cannot be afforded. The active enforcement and more particularly the judicial enforcement of these liberties is seen by them, for the present at any rate, as an undesirable and often unpredictable fetter upon the ability of the state to provide essential amenities and security.

Often, too, in discussion with practical politicians, one finds that doubts concerning the constitutional guarantee of liberty are pressed to even more fundamental levels. I have known several African intellectuals raise the question whether, in essence, the classical constitutional limitations presuppose and, indeed, buttress economic individualism, which may or may not be acceptable in the particular new society with which one is concerned, however fundamental the concept may be in most Western democracies. In short, there is influential support for the view that "the demands of security must take precedence over the demands for liberty in respect of the minimum human needs," which, incidentally, is the conclusion that Humuyun Kabir himself reached.[55]

[55] *Id.* at 193.

Here, then, is a fundamental issue, a great challenge, now being fought out with particular urgency in Africa. Can it be demonstrated that the democratic procedures, and the legal institutions which have protected civil liberty in the West, are in fact capable of adjustment so as to accommodate the clamant need of new nations for rapid economic growth without losing their essential character in the process of accommodation and adaptation?

While I do not for one moment deny the great importance of providing social and economic security, I do utterly repudiate the notion that the provision of these benefits should be given pride of place above all other freedoms. In fact, as I see it, we are faced here with one of the deepest issues between Russia and her satellites on the one hand, and the would-be free world on the other.

Under the Russian system the state claims to be the universal provider, with the result that the individual ceases to count at all. This, in my view, is deeply immoral; for though there are many services which the state should undertake for men, its prime duty is to create the conditions which permit its members to act freely within the law for themselves. Indeed a state which purports to be a universal provider actually wrongs men by treating them contrary to their nature; for a man's first duty is to fulfill his nature by assuming the responsibilities that are his.

But quite apart from the moral ground to which I have referred, there are two very practical reasons why individual men and women should, as far as possible, be allowed to work out their own destiny free from state control and interference. In the first place, once the state's claim to be a universal provider is acknowledged or encouraged, it is very difficult to resist a further claim on its part to regiment men, as indeed the history of communist Russia has proved. Moreover, human beings are fallible, and no man or group of men is good enough to be entrusted with absolute power over other men. Indeed, this is perhaps the decisive justification for reversible democratic government and for the freedom implicit in it to organize opposition.

At the same time it is not sufficient merely to reject totalitarianism and fulminate against communism. It is no less necessary to guard against the misuse of private enterprise. Otherwise, one merely avoids one kind of slavery to fall victim to another.

Under communism the means of production are controlled by the officers of the state, who are the masters of the workers (that is to say, the slaves of the state), and the wealth produced is distributed, at the discretion of state officials, among families and individuals. At the other extreme—which is in my view equally pernicious—you have unbridled private enterprise. This is the mark of what Hilaire Belloc, that stern foe of communism, called "The Servile State."

But we are not necessarily doomed to suffer either of these grim ways. Elsewhere I have argued that between the extremes of unbridled private enterprise, or economic license, on the one hand, and state despotism on the other, there is a middle way, where it is possible to combine freedom for all with a necessary minimum of economic benefit, opportunity and security for all, especially within the fields of public health and education.[56] Elsewhere, too, I have ventured to give my reasons for believing that the basic human freedoms are not irreconcilable with rapid economic growth in underdeveloped countries.[57] I do not propose to elaborate these views here beyond saying two things.

In the first place, we should, I think, have no sympathy with those who would attempt to force African realities Procrustes-fashion into Western political and economic molds and who criticize newly independent African states on the ground that their polities are not exact replicas of Western systems. Let us remember that in trying to make an adjustment between welfare and personal freedom, the new nations of Africa are faced with what must always be a very delicate problem of balance, but which, currently in Africa, is exceptionally difficult. In their attempts to meet this challenge they need sympathy and help rather than too impatient criticism.

Secondly, there can be little doubt that in the difficult task of establishing and maintaining what I have called the middle way, the law has a big role. For example, laws preventing the abuse of economic power—among them, anti-monopoly laws—can do much to help. But in themselves, laws of this kind are not enough, for ultimately the institution of private property and free individual enterprise must rest, not on greed or the will to win a rat-race, or on some sloppy economic optimism that all happens for the best in the best of all possible worlds, but on a developed sense of moral responsibility among the general body of citizens.

Let us, however, pause on this idea of moral responsibility, for it brings us to the fundamental challenge which Africa presents to the rest of the world. Superficially, one might question whether a continent as underdeveloped as Africa has any challenge to offer to the old established nations, and especially to the West with its great heritage of accomplishment. But a moment's reflection should dissipate any such illusion.

The African challenge has, in the view of many, become highlighted by the East-West struggle, by the Cold War; but it is essential to realize that the New Africa does not wish to be a mere passive entity to be carved up between Russia and the Western Alliance in a new, more subtle, era of colonialism, a colonialism of economic influence and political ideology. The New Africa is determined, whatever the cost, to be itself, to win self-confidence, and to resolve its own problems in its own way.

A short while ago Mr. Tom Mboya of Kenya brought these points into very clear focus in a television interview in Chicago. He was asked where he, and African nationalists generally, stood in the great struggle now going on between Russia and the United States, more particularly between Russia and the Western

[56] D. V. COWEN, LIBERTY, EQUALITY, FRATERNITY—TODAY (The Hoernlé Memorial Lecture, Institute of Race Relations, Johannesburg, 1961); D. V. COWEN, THE FOUNDATIONS OF FREEDOM (1961).
[57] See the works cited *supra* note 56.

Alliance. He replied that African nationalists generally stood for a policy of non-alignment with either the Western or the Eastern bloc. Africans preferred, he said, to exercise an uncommitted and impartial judgment strictly in accordance with the merits of each issue, rather than by reference to who the contesting parties might be.

Reminded of the perplexity which many westerners feel when faced with this attitude of non-alignment or "positive neutralism"—a perplexity which has been summed up in the question "How can you be neutral in a conflict between good and evil"—Mr. Mboya began to develop a most powerful challenge.

Africans, he said, were by no means indifferent to moral issues. While in no way committed to Russian policies, particularly Russian communism, Africans, he suggested, could not accept that the West was a paragon of virtue to be followed blindly at all times on all issues. To expect Africans to judge international issues on an either-or basis, and solely in terms of the East-West conflict, was in his view not only arrogant but unreasonably limiting. By the same token, he would not expect Americans to fetter their judgment and limit their vision by choosing to be either "Western Alliance Firsters" or, alternatively, "Africa Firsters." Rather, he would expect an adult American, when asked the question (recently posed in an influential journal)[58] "Which friends come first—the New Africa or the Old Europe in NATO?" to answer "It depends on the issue." On fundamentals, like equal protection of the law regardless of color, the issue should, he felt, be decisive: there was a right and a wrong, and wrong could not become right because one's old or new friends espoused it.

Pressed a little harder, Mr. Mboya proceeded to throw out what I regard as the really fundamental challenge. In effect he said: "We Africans are often perplexed by the West's own confusion. Just what is it that you in the West do stand for?"

There is irony here and a most salutary lesson. Africa is sometimes viewed in the West as a "primitive" continent. Yet it is this continent which is demanding of the West that it rediscover itself, that it recall and rethink and re-apply its cultural, moral, and spiritual principles.

And indeed who can doubt that all is not well with the West. There is, in fact, an ominous parallel between the later years of the Roman Empire and our own times. To quote St. Gregory, while superficially the world flourished, "in men's hearts it had already withered—*in cordibus aruerat.*" Similarly today, despite man's technical achievements, there is inner doubt and tension and a groping for values and meaningfulness which mock at the achievements themselves.

If the West believes that it has anything to offer other than technology and a high degree of material comfort, it is urgent that besides training engineers and doctors, it be able to interpret the ideals of good government which it professes to stand for, and unfold the heart of the philosophy on which those ideals rest. But before people can justify their beliefs to others, they must be able to justify them to themselves.

[58] White, *Which Friends Come First?*, Harper's Magazine, March 1962, p. 100.

We set much store upon safeguarding the rights of the individual human being, and very rightly so. But to talk about human rights and human dignity without comprehending human nature in its metaphysical dimension is meaningless, and so to comprehend it means to see that human rights must be related to that moral law which is rooted in being itself.

In a notable book, entitled "We Hold These Truths,"[59] Father John Courtney Murray has said that "the trouble is that even a damnable philosophy is more effective than no philosophy at all." The West, then, must rediscover itself. And those who value freedom, equality, and brotherhood, as opposed to communism or any other totalitarian system, must cleave to the heart of the philosophy on which these values depend. We must ask again the question which, of all questions, catalyzed the development of Western civilization: What is man, and what are the purposes which give meaning to his existence? And we must never lose sight of that question.

It is a vain and idle belief that all one has to do in order to build a stable and just society is to call in the right constitution-makers, economists, and sociologists. The finest constitutions, the most carefully devised Bills of Rights, are but scraps of paper in the wind if the people who work them, and for whom they are meant, are not worthy of them. No amount of economic aid, no program of social reform, can avail a society where the individuals who comprise it have lost sight of the nature of man and the function of society itself. Certainly constitutional guarantees and Bills of Rights (about which there is so much talk in contemporary Africa) are likely to be very shaky affairs unless men are agreed upon the philosophical basis on which these fundamental rights rest.

In this regard Jacques Maritain has observed that, from the point of view of philosophic doctrine, it may be said that in regard to human rights men are today divided into two groups: those who to a greater or lesser extent explicitly accept and those who to a greater or lesser extent explicitly reject natural law as the basis of those rights. In the eye of the first, the requirements of his being endow man with certain fundamental and inalienable rights antecedent in nature and superior to society. These are the source of social life itself and of the duties and rights which it implies. For the second school, man's rights are constantly variable and in a state of flux, being *entirely* the product of society as it advances with the forward march of history.[60]

The consequences of accepting one of these points of view rather than the other are great; for it can, I think, be demonstrated that without the sense of direction given to a society by an understanding of the natural law, and man's place within its framework, power and expediency can become the highest arbiters of behavior and of the enactments of the state, leaving the way wide open for dictators and authoritarian governments on the premise that might is right.

[59] JOHN COURTNEY MURRAY, WE HOLD THESE TRUTHS 91 (1960).
[60] Jacques Maritain, *Introduction* to HUMAN RIGHTS, COMMENTS AND INTERPRETATIONS—A SYMPOSIUM 13 (UNESCO, 1949).

It is beyond the scope of this paper to attempt this demonstration;[61] nor is it possible here to spell out what is meant by "natural law" in the Aristotelian-Thomistic tradition—the version which alone would seem to be clear in regard to basic principles, while giving full recognition to the importance of the actual experience of time and place.[62]

I have raised the issue of natural law here, not to ride a hobbyhorse, but because it cleaves to the heart of the subject with which we are concerned. Sooner or later in any really serious discussion of human rights and their protection, the foundations of the subject will be probed, as anyone with any experience of lecturing to a critical African (or, indeed, any critical) audience knows well. At that point lawyers may perhaps be forgiven for not being adherents of natural law in the Aristotelian-Thomistic tradition, but it is less pardonable if their condition is based on an assured and glassy ignorance, on equating Rousseau with, say, St. Thomas, or John Locke with Hooker, or Descartes with Socrates (Karl Popper to the contrary notwithstanding).

E. International Legal Studies

The themes we are now discussing are, of course, related also to the fifth of the broad topics which I suggested earlier might be of dominant interest throughout the African continent, namely, international relations and legal studies. Here again, a generous and humane approach is needed. Apart from courses on what may be called international law in the traditional sense, that is to say, the subject which lawyers of my generation studied at some time in the pages of, say, Oppenheim or Hall, attention must plainly be given to the legal aspects of international banking, business, and investment; to international organization and agencies for cooperation; to the international aspects of various forms of constitutional structure (for example, international voting rights in various federal or quasi-federal associations); to the ramifications of the European Common Market; and to the emergence of comparable organizations in Africa.

Questions concerning the minimum legal requirements for the working of an effective common market, and more especially the minimum of "uniformity" or "harmonization" that may be required among the legal systems of the countries comprising a common market, are of ever-increasing importance not only in Europe but, in an intimately related way, in Africa and elsewhere.[63]

But all this is familiar enough, and will not escape attention; it is necessary, however, to go deeper. The notion of state sovereignty, which has so often stood

---

[61] For an admirably lucid statement of the essentials, see JOHN WILD, PLATO'S MODERN ENEMIES AND THE THEORY OF NATURAL LAW (1953). Professor Wild deals, *inter alia*, with the epistemological and the metaphysical foundations of the subject, with the significance of contingent propositions, and especially with the Aristotelian idea of nature as a process of becoming—essential topics which lawyers not infrequently overlook in discussions of natural law.

[62] See generally, GEORGES RENARD, LE DROIT, LA JUSTICE ET LA VOLONTÉ (1924); GEORGES RENARD, LE DROIT, L'ORDRE ET LA RAISON (1927).

[63] Luchaire, *Le maintien et le renouvellement de l'association des États d'Afrique et de Madagascar au Marché Commun*, in Penant, April/May, 1961, pp. 185-99.

in the way of creating a world order of peace and justice among the older nations, is a source of perplexity, too, among the new African nations. All over the continent today political leaders are interested in plans for the closer association of states on a Pan-African basis—plans which hold out much of promise for future economic development and military defense. But always there lurks the danger of their coming to grief because of a reluctance on the part of states to surrender to a supranational organization any part of their newly-won sovereignty.[64]

It is possible that the desired economic and military objectives may be achieved in Africa without resorting to federalism of the classical kind, that is to say, without any effective loss of sovereignty by the associating states, a contention put forward in a very interesting paper by M. Gabriel d'Arboussier, of Senegal, at the Symposium on Federalism in the New Nations held in the Law School of the University of Chicago in February 1962.[65] Others, however, are less sanguine about averting the sovereignty issue; and it is perhaps significant that in some African constitutions— notably that of Ghana—provision is made for the eventual surrender of sovereignty in the interests of Pan-African solidarity. Time alone will show how effective this may prove to be.

F. Legal Education

Africans are today deeply concerned with the kind of legal education which they should foster. That purely technical courses will miss the mark is evident. At the same time the need is urgent in several parts of Africa to train lawyers quickly for the day-to-day run of legal work. Years of neglect have, in some territories, resulted in a dearth of legally qualified Africans.[66] Several subjects of a more scholarly and reflective kind may therefore, for the time being, have to be excluded from curricula of comparatively short duration which may be deemed sufficient to qualify for junior professional work and even for junior judicial work. At the same time, African needs will not be sufficiently met by routine training of a purely technical kind.

As we have seen, African lawyers and statesmen are increasingly being called upon to make decisions on legal problems which have basic and most far-reaching social and economic significance; they cannot afford to make these decisions without a liberal education, including, in particular, acquaintance with the previous experience of other peoples who have had to face similar problems.

African lawyers will fail in the exacting tasks which lie before them unless their education is conceived in the grand manner and aims at being truly fundamental, truly philosophical. However short of the goal one might fall in legal education, one

---

[64] Compare the reluctance of the states of the Netherlands to enter into anything more than a loose confederation after winning liberation from the Spain of Phillip II, with the recent amendments of the Netherlands Constitution so as to give precedence to international agreements.

[65] I am at present editing the papers and proceedings; publication is expected in 1963.

[66] I understand that in Tanganyika today (May 1962) there are only four Africans who have professional legal qualifications. An African friend once remarked that this is partly attributable to the fact that students choosing, for example, agriculture and medicine were, in colonial days, given greater encouragement on the ground that lawyers were troublemakers rather than trouble-shooters.

must aim high. And nowhere is this more imperative than in the law schools of the new nations. It was for this reason that in a public lecture which I delivered at the University of Chicago in April 1959, I advocated the inclusion of comparative law, jurisprudence, and legal history in any realistically conceived curriculum of African legal studies. My colleague, Professor Max Rheinstein, was and still is receptive to the idea, but the general opinion at the time was that "first things should come first," and that the first need in Africa is basic legal training of a bread-and-butter kind.

However, elementary legal training of a more or less technical kind for the many is not incompatible with the concurrent provision of something more ambitious. The concurrent establishment of research institutes attached to the new African law schools would surely not weaken them. On the contrary, it might enhance their capacity to discharge essential teaching duties.

II

The American Contribution

What can American institutions and American legal scholars usefully hope to contribute and achieve in the field of African studies? Perhaps the first and most essential fact to take into account is that African legal studies are at present, and for some considerable time are likely to remain, in a state of flux. Dramatic and rapid change is the dominant fact almost everywhere on the African continent; indeed in some places the much-publicized winds of change have now reached hurricane force. This naturally has an intimate bearing on the nature and possibilities of significant academic work in this field. Pieces of purely descriptive writing on, for example, the constitutional structure of particular African countries, and attempts at constitution-making, have a disquieting tendency to be out of date almost as soon as they are published or completed. Nevertheless, however frustrating it may be to be overtaken and left behind by the march of events, work of this descriptive and practical kind is important and must be undertaken.

Again, within the general field of legal education and research, it would seem that during this period of rapid change and growth, research projects, teaching methods, and especially the organization and content of courses and seminars, should remain flexible, and—for some time—largely exploratory and experimental. And for this reason, I have hesitated to put forward any ideas on the subject at all, especially as a newcomer in a country which has proved itself to be so fertile in resource. Nevertheless, I have ventured to put together a few tentative ideas, and these are here set forth briefly.

First, a note of warning against over-indulgence in missionary zeal. I would not dream of disparaging the present experiment of sending American legal scholars to African law schools to help build them up. On the contrary, it would seem that this endeavor is of considerable potential value and is being welcomed in Africa itself. Nor would I presume to suggest that the distinguished gentlemen who have volunteered to do this exacting work—among them Professor W. B. Harvey of the University of Michigan, now Dean of the University Law Department and Director of Legal Education of Ghana—are not fully aware of what I am about to say. But for the possible benefit of the less sophisticated I would make this plea: let us be careful to keep our feet on solid earth.

It has sometimes been suggested, almost in hushed tones, that there is missionwork for lawyers in this field, that lawyers imbued with Western values may carry the light, so to speak, into the darknesses of Africa, and save it from communism and other forms of totalitarianism. This is not only pathetically naïve but positively harmful. It is naïve because if any generalization about Africa, as a whole, can safely be made, it is this: Africans desire complete and unfettered freedom to be themselves; to build up their self-confidence and make their own distinctive contribution, in their own way, to the art of living and social organization. It is harmful, because they will reject anything savoring of what I have heard one of them describe as "cultural imperialism," with no less vigor and angry contempt than that with which they have already rejected political and economic imperialism. And needless to say, they will deeply resent, and rightly resent, any hint of being patronized.

Let us be quite clear, then, that one will get absolutely nowhere in the new nations field if one embarks upon it after prejudging the issues and with inflexible preconceptions about the role of law and legal institutions. *Semper aliquid novi ex Africa* is likely to be as true in the field of law as it has been in other fields.

Rather than deceive ourselves with grandiose schemes about missionizing, we should be humble enough to remember, and this is my second point, that teaching is a two-way process, in which the teacher, if he is wise, is given an opportunity to learn as much as he teaches. For example, anyone teaching constitutional law in Africa would do well to remember that the idea of constitutionalism is no novelty among Africans, and that indigenous African institutions have much to teach in regard to the taming of power.[67] No one would seriously suggest that the old ways of disciplining tyrannous chiefs are fully applicable in a modern state, but modern techniques are often only means of achieving ancient objectives; and it helps greatly to give them vitality and acceptability if it can be shown that, despite their modern garb, they are really old friends.

In a deep sense, of course—a very deep sense—there is mission work to do, namely, the work of rediscovering and articulating, right here among established Western communities, the real foundations of our own most cherished values. In the long run, the values which are sometimes described as the "Western" way of life, the values of human dignity and limited government in a free society, can only survive *anywhere* if those who subscribe to them are able to give sound and convincing reasons as to why they do so; as to why these values are good and right.

---

[67] The point has been emphasized by almost every informed writer on African institutions. See, for example, JOHN MACLEAN, A COMPENDIUM OF KAFIR LAWS AND CUSTOMS 24 (1858); and among more recent writings, I. SCHAPERA, GOVERNMENT AND POLITICS IN TRIBAL SOCIETIES 135 (1956).

And this is precisely what scholars in the new nations field, especially in Africa, are so often challenged to do.

Let it be remembered, too, that in working back from contemporary needs and application in the new nations to the relevance of established Western and other institutions as potential sources of guidance, and in explaining established institutions to the peoples of new nations, who may desire, where practicable, to imitate successes and avoid mistakes, the scholar in the new nations field is given a golden opportunity to learn afresh, and with the stimulus of actuality, the true inwardness of much that we take for granted and allow, at our peril, to go unanalyzed. In short, the virtue of the exercise lies as much in what may be gained by the established nations, through looking again at the foundations of their own life, as in what may be given to the new nations. In this regard, the potential fillip that may be given to such subjects as constitutional law and government, general jurisprudence, public international law, and conflict of laws, can hardly be exaggerated.

Thirdly, I would like to elaborate a little on possible American programs within the field of African legal studies. At the outset, I would stress again the importance of remaining flexible and experimental; for there is very little experience anywhere to guide us, and over-elaborate, long-term commitments in particular schools may prove both costly and abortive. At the same time there are certain minimum requirements which, it is submitted, should be satisfied before any law school may fairly be said to be seriously interested in African legal studies, and presently I shall try to indicate what these requirements are.

Several possible approaches to African legal studies suggest themselves:

1. Some schools may prefer to confine themselves to introducing a little African material by way of illustration or illumination in subjects such as jurisprudence, constitutional law, administrative law, land-use, and problems of international commerce and investment—all of these courses continuing to be offered as part of the established curriculum for an ordinary American degree (probably on an elective basis). There would certainly be nothing novel about this procedure. It would not necessarily involve additions of staff, though perhaps a few seemingly strange tomes may have to be added in those sections of law libraries which are sometimes imperially reserved for "Anglo-American legal treatises." Possibly the librarian might be persuaded to set aside a section of the shelf space for a small collection of books on African law. But, however one looks at this first approach, it could hardly be described as a serious venture in African legal studies.

2. Other schools may choose to edge warily somewhat further into the field. They may do this by the recruitment to their staff of one or more persons with some special knowledge of African legal studies; by organizing one or more courses of instruction with an African focus; by encouraging African graduate students to pursue a course of study in the law school; by sponsoring African research projects; and by a serious attempt to build up comprehensive library facilities in African law.

For example, in the Law School of the University of Chicago the first steps have been taken to offer a seminar or course on African legal problems, the focus of the exercise being (a) to identify and discuss some of the main legal "problem areas" in Africa; and (b) to consider how much of American legal experience is relevant and capable of adaptation in Africa. A not dissimilar course had for some time been offered by Professor Arthur Schiller at the Columbia Law School.

Work of this kind is, in my view, a high priority. Thus, apart from its intrinsic interest, it may help to throw light on what is actually needed, as well as on what one may hope to accomplish, in the field of African legal studies.[68] Moreover, it may not be without relevance to the work of directors of graduate studies in the United States, for there is a risk that African students in America may miss taking courses which are of value in their own country and, conversely, give time to those which prove to be of purely domestic interest.

It hardly needs demonstration that American ideas in the field of constitutional law, to give a clear example, are of great interest in contemporary Africa. It would therefore seem logical to offer, as at Chicago, a course or courses on comparative constitutional and administrative law, with a substantial but by no means exclusively African focus. In addition, courses on such subjects as international law, international trade and investment, and the Common Market, could easily be adapted to take in or emphasize topics of particular African interest.

While instruction of this kind plainly has something to offer to postgraduate students from Africa, it should perhaps be emphasized that equal benefit may accrue to American students, especially those contemplating work in the new nations.

Assume the presence of four or five good postgraduate students from African countries in a law school offering such a program,[69] and one has what I would describe as "the beginnings of a center of African legal studies." But courses and seminars of this kind are only the beginnings. Much more is needed if the "center" is to survive and make the kind of contribution which should be made. Among these additional requirements, I would enumerate specifically the following:

(a) building up a library containing the major African legal materials. This is, of course, a very costly and difficult undertaking, for many items other than strictly legal ones should be made easily accessible, and the whole collection should be brought together in a special section of the library. Again, quite apart from the questions of cost and library organization, much of the essential material is out of print. But the difficulties are not insuperable, and it is still possible over a period of, say, five to ten years, to build up major collections of African legal (and complementary) materials in perhaps four or five big

---

[68] Thanks largely to the enthusiasm and dedicated work of a fine body of students, this was made manifest to the present author in the first seminar course of this kind offered by the University of Chicago during the winter of 1962.

[69] Again, it is at present the policy of the Law School in the University of Chicago to assist good African students at the post graduate level.

centers in the United States. Indeed, substantial collections are already in existence in the libraries of several American law schools, and some of them could with little trouble be developed so as to become really great collections;[70]

(b) provision of facilities for uninterrupted research and publication. In due course African universities and African research institutes will, one hopes, have the library and other resources to embark in full measure on major research in African legal studies. And in due course, too, one hopes, they will play—and certainly they should be encouraged to play—the leading role in this field. But there are at present few such institutions,[71] though the need for them grows daily more urgent. It is here, I think, that the bigger centers of learning in America might make one of their more important contributions. A comparatively small staff of academic collaborators, say, four men well acquainted with African conditions,[72] who are given time and favorable conditions to do basic research, could do work which might not only be an addition to scholarship, but which might also be esteemed in Africa as as contribution towards the solution of the many problems which there present themselves. Indeed, in this latter regard, it should not be overlooked that in the formative years, while centers of higher legal learning and research are finding their feet among the new nations of Africa, research projects which are based abroad may have a certain advantage by the very fact of detachment.

3. A far more elaborate venture would be the establishment of a school of African and Oriental Studies along the lines of the London prototype, in which law would be one part of the program, the whole being affiliated, more or less closely, to a university. It is possible that one or more of those American universities which already have well-established centers of African studies in the fields of anthropology or political science may wish to develop along these lines.[73]

4. Some of the major centers may prefer to integrate African legal studies into the work of large Institutes of Comparative Law, or centers of International Legal Studies, associated with the law school, and indeed with the university as a whole, but separately housed and with some measure of financial and other autonomy. This approach could be very fruitful indeed, but it is, of course, far more ambitious and costly than the kind of "step-by-step" venture discussed above.

Fourthly, I would suggest that in developing the American contribution, one should not become bogged down by attempts to force "African legal studies" into fixed categories, such as "area studies," or "comparative and foreign law," or "international legal studies," and so on. Discussions along these lines seem to engender

---

[70] The collection at Harvard is probably already in this category, or very near it.

[71] South Africa with its comparatively long and diversified university experience is, perhaps, in a special category.

[72] Including an expert on the various Islamic rites in Africa. See, generally, J. N. D. ANDERSON, THE FUTURE OF ISLAMIC LAW IN AFRICA (1954).

[73] There are already a substantial number of such centers in the United States, among them Northwestern University, Johns Hopkins, the University of California, Boston University, and the Massachusetts Institute of Technology.

more heat than light, however useful a particular label may be for fund-raising. In a sense, African legal studies may be embraced under any of these rubrics, though in my view the great range of legal systems involved in Africa and the diversity of that enormous Continent make "African law" far less of a unified and manageable "area study" than, say, Chinese, Japanese, or Russian legal studies. No doubt, when the legal problem areas of Africa have been properly identified, various institutions may be depended upon to choose their own categorizations to suit their own purposes. Meanwhile it appears to be more important to obtain clarity about what one means by "African legal studies," and to get on with the actual and pressing job of doing work in the field.

Fifthly, I would like to call attention to the very special importance which attaches to interdisciplinary cooperation. For example, a lawyer embarking on a project for the improvement of land tenure without the assistance of a competent social anthropologist to explain the ramifications of various legislative proposals on, say, the position of the chieftainship (which may rest on power to allocate land), is likely to find that his carefully devised plans will never reach the point of "take-off." Then, again, even a potentially workable plan has to be popularized. In this regard, in addition to the skills of the social anthropologist and perhaps the social psychologist, one cannot afford to ignore the contribution which may be made by the practical administrator who is in touch with day-to-day realities.

In the African field it is particularly important to learn the idiom—not necessarily the language (desirable as this may be)—of the people with whom one is dealing. One must make an effort to grasp the concepts and images with which they are familiar. If one is, for example, to explain American realities to Africans, this must be done in language, and with the help of concepts and idiom, which is meaningful to Africans, and *vice versa*. The "judicial process," for example, among the Lozi in Barotseland is not the same phenomenon as the judicial process in the state of Illinois, and it may not be helpful to expound either in terms of the other. Greater facility in communication is one of the many advantages which interdisciplinary cooperation, especially between lawyers, social anthropologists, economists, and political scientists, may bring in its train.

But most of this is familiar to all but the veriest tyro and is not likely to be forgotten. And so I come to my sixth and last point, one which is no less obvious, perhaps, than the need for interdisciplinary cooperation, but which in the excitement of new ventures might sometimes tend to be forgotten. I refer to the need for law teachers in the various universities working in the new nations field to cooperate among themselves as scholars whose first allegiance should be to the task of expanding the frontiers of knowledge and usefulness, and helping each other to do so. This applies not only to relations between American universities, but also, and perhaps particularly, to Anglo-American, Franco-American, and Afro-American relations in this field.

The subject is worthwhile, potentially even great. It behooves us to be worthy of it.

PERSONNEL PROBLEMS IN THE ADMINISTRATION OF JUSTICE IN NIGERIA

Sir Adetokunbo Ademola[*]

Since the year 1955, the personnel problems in the administration of justice in Nigeria have become more and more complex. From one particular angle, to which I shall have cause to refer later, the problems will in about ten years' time become more and more acute. Before 1955, Nigeria had what can be called a unified judiciary. There was one Chief Justice for the whole country, with a number of puisne judges under him, as well as magistrates, registrars, and the clerical staff. Judges and magistrates were recruited from the Colonial Judicial Service. Many of them were expatriates, with a good number of Africans. The registrars and the clerical staff have always been Africans. Every member of the staff under the Chief Justice, be he a judge, a magistrate, a registrar, or on the clerical staff, was expected to serve in any part of Nigeria; and so it was that a judge who served one year in Lagos or in Western Nigeria would find himself in the North or in the East the following year.

When it was decided that Nigeria should adopt a federal form of government, there were some—particularly in the judiciary—who advocated that the judiciary should not be regionalized and that a unitary judiciary should continue to serve the country. The politicians, however, thought otherwise, and the view taken was that if the country was to be regionalized, it must be a full regionalization including the judiciary. The argument that a unitary judiciary would serve to bind the different regions or states together more closely was dismissed, and the country was harnessed for a regionalized judiciary.

The first difficulty the department had to encounter was the distribution of staff to the three different Regions and to Lagos. By the end of 1955, however, everybody's nose was at the grindstone in his Region, and all was well.

1. *Personnel*

The machinery of justice works with many wheels. Quite apart from judges and magistrates, many more are employed in the administration of justice; and their duties vary as does their status. There are the Registrars in different grades, the Sheriff, the Director of Prisons, and their clerical and other staff, and this is by no means an exhaustive list. Their position or responsibility, high or low as it may be, is not to be taken as a conclusive index to their importance in the general scheme of the administration of justice. The ordinary court interpreter can be a veritable factor for miscarriage of justice, if he chooses to be corrupt.

[*] B.A. (Hons.) 1931, M.A. (Hons.) 1934, Cambridge University, Honorary Bencher of the Middle Temple, Barrister at Law. Chief Justice of the Federation, Federal Supreme Court of Nigeria, since 1958.

The judge—and the magistrate, of course—is the central figure in the scheme of things; and around him the whole machinery of justice revolves. If he is careful and conscientious, very little can go amiss because not only is he charged with the duty of decision making but the administrative machinery must be supervised carefully by him, unless, of course, he is in the headquarters. There, the Chief Justice himself is personally responsible for the administrative machinery. In this supervisory capacity, he is helped by a high officer known as the Chief Registrar, whose office is higher than that of a magistrate.

In a country with a written constitution like Nigeria, the judge occupies such a unique position as the arbiter of rights and duties, not only between citizen and citizen but also between the state and the citizen, and in a federal constitution, it may be added, as between the constituent regional states.

2. *Requisites of a good judge*

I have mentioned earlier the unique position of a judge in a country with a written constitution; this is more marked in a newly independent country. But however good and however democratic the constitution may appear to be, it has, in the last resort, to depend and be greatly influenced by the quality of its judges who have to give it interpretation. The more detached or impersonal the judge, the more likely will the intention of the framers of the constitution fructify.

This, of course, raises the all-important problem of recruitment. In this respect three important aspects have to be considered:

(i) the general problem of criteria on recruitment;
(ii) the problem of specialization and allocation;
(iii) the problem of efficiency and promotion.

In considering the general problem of criteria and selection, it must be borne in mind that the colonial powers have left behind in their former colonies their tradition and conception of justice. This has without doubt affected, to a large degree, the outlook on criteria. What are those qualities which make a good judge; what do you look for in a judge? That there is a unanimity of opinion on this cannot be doubted, although these qualities may be enhanced or impaired depending upon methods adopted in recruiting judges.

The basic qualities of a good judge are:

(a) Sound knowledge of the law. This hardly needs any amplification. A sound logical mind helps in the assimilation of this knowledge.
(b) The matter of detachment. A good judge should be objective in assessing facts. A judge should never allow his own personal feelings or his own preconceived notions to displace facts which have been proved before him.
(c) Sound common sense. It should be accepted that not all matters which come before a judge need only knowledge of the law. A judge must also be good

on facts and his assessment of facts, *i.e.*, evaluation of the evidence before him and deductions from facts. Common sense is an indispensable factor in the attributes of a good judge.

(d) A judge should be humane. This attribute, to my mind, plays an important role in the relation between the judiciary and the public. The humane element in the administration of justice has always strengthened the position of the judiciary in any country.

(e) Freedom from fear, prejudice, or corruption. Modern constitutions provide for the appointment, renewal of appointment, dismissal, general welfare, and promotion of judges; freedom from political or other influences are also of paramount importance.

Judges are paid reasonably good salaries in order to minimize the possibility of corruption. No matter how many freedoms there are, however, the determining factor indeed is the character of the judge himself.

The Nigerian outlook on recruitment is at present basically English. Whether this will change or not, it is difficult to say, but it is obvious that for some years this will remain so. A judge should be a lawyer with a reasonably long practice, sufficient to enable those among whom he functions to be able to assess the above qualities. There is something to be said in favor of the democratic system of election of judges in some of the states in the United States of America, but my view is that this is not likely to work in Nigeria; the man who wins an election is likely to have the least of the qualities already enumerated. What is more, there is also the grave danger of having to please supporters or sometimes the temptation of allowing the prospects of future election to interfere with the administration of justice. I have heard a judge from the United States say that he did not have to bother for the next three years, but after that time he must start to think of his future; it was no doubt said with humor and in jest, but such a position will undoubtedly not appeal to the African mind.

The method of selection may theoretically seem to be less democratic, but it appears to be on the whole a better system. The politicians are not in sympathy generally with any system which excludes their right to determine, but they always have a good word for an impartial judiciary.

3. *The problem of specialization and allocation*

Views differ as to whether judges should specialize, or whether the judicial system itself should departmentalize. On the whole, it is true that the legal knowledge and experience required of judges in the following courts are not the same: criminal court, civil court, land court, constitutional court, industrial court, and international court.

In medicine today, it is important to specialize, and it may be that one day we shall find very few general practitioners about. When the time comes that there is a dearth of general practitioners, the swing in that direction will undoubtedly start. In law, the general practitioner will for many years to come in Nigeria be the order of the day. In England, where a lawyer chooses early in his career whether he will practice in the chancery or the common law side, or in the criminal courts, it is easier from time to time to be in a position to appoint judges who are masters of, or who specialize in, different departments of the law. This undoubtedly makes for efficiency. When I visited a firm of legal practitioners in New York, I found no less than twenty-four lawyers, all specialists, each in his own branch of the law. A client who consults has his matter dealt with by a member of the firm suitable to his case. This is still unknown in Nigeria, where there are but few cases of partnership. It is hoped many more partnerships will spring or grow up. But even then, for the present, in Nigeria, a client consults a particular barrister because he is Mr. X, known to him in one way or another. He certainly does not wish his case handled by any other barrister but that barrister of his choice.

As with barristers, it is the same with judges in Nigeria. A judge does not specialize; he is trained to handle any case which comes before him; he has no choice. The Nigerian Constitution undoubtedly is somewhat complex. With the complex Federal Constitution, the problem of specialization for the Bench as well as the Bar may come earlier than expected; it is evident that a few lawyers are taking particular interest in constitutional matters before the courts. A "body of opinion" may soon grow up in that direction; a good few members of the Bar would specialize in Constitutional Law. This, to my mind, is frightfully important in a country with a written constitution. With specialization from the Bar, the Bench will have to think quickly. Specialization in Nigeria, however, is not likely to be on a large scale; it will be no more than in constitutional law and international law. It is doubtful if a separate Constitutional Court, as in Germany, will be introduced in Nigeria in the foreseeable future.

4. *Problems of efficiency and promotion*

Important considerations enter into this, particularly where, as in Nigeria, the judiciary is regionalized. Each Region tends to prefer the natives of the Region, and the problem is how to reconcile this fact with efficiency and a sense of responsibility. There is no doubt that an efficient judge who is a native of a Region is more likely to understand the psychology of his "locals" and thereby to have a distinct advantage over the others. But there is a definite threat to the impartial administration of justice from our undue stress of geographical or ethnological qualification for the Bench.

Similarly, there is the desire to give effect to the federal texture in a place like Nigeria through a mixed composition of the judiciary in Lagos, particularly in the Federal Supreme Court. This may be desirable—I myself doubt it—but it may easily be overstressed. It raises the problem that in an attempt to mix the Court, the best judges would not necessarily be promoted to the Federal Supreme Court. Allied to this is the problem of promotion from the lower Bench (magistrates) to the

Bench (judgeship). It certainly will be a sad thing for Nigeria at present to attempt in any way to indulge in mixing any of the courts in the federal territory of Lagos. It seems reasonably certain that for the present the problem of a Mixed Court is not likely to gain favor with the Bar and with the people. I am well aware that a few people are not only thinking about it but are already talking about it. The idea will not, however, germinate, for the present, for reasons already mentioned; also because there are not as many qualified candidates in one or two of the Regions. In other parts of the world where the federal structure is reflected on the Bench, it has not produced a better result than the system of letting the best man have the job. This problem, I daresay, will be more and more difficult as the Federation gets older.

5. *Problems due to regionalization*

Regionalization of the judiciary has also brought in its wake the question of uniform standards. The Western Region of Nigeria—particularly that part of the West nearer to Lagos—and Lagos have produced three generations of lawyers. In the Eastern Region, there is an old, established bar in the very small town of Calabar, but otherwise present lawyers are the first generation at the bar. The Northern Region has only just started but it is running very fast in the race. Therefore, of the thousand legal practitioners in Nigeria, a great number are from the Western Region and Lagos.

So far there has not been any inter-regional transfer of judges. There is no reason why this should not happen; it might be easy in one or two Regions, but owing to the centrifugal tendencies of regional legislation, it may prove rather difficult in the future with some Regions.

6. *Unified Judicial System in Pan-African World*

The tendency to unify everything African is prevalent; it has been considered that a unification of the judicial system in Africa will be ideal. This is not going to be an easy matter. There is the problem of language which will undoubtedly be a stumbling block, quite apart from the difference in the judicial systems in the English-speaking territories in Africa and in the French-speaking territories.

These are but a few personnel problems in the administration of justice in Nigeria; they are not insurmountable. With the ability of the Nigerians to laugh at their own mistakes, and with our natural humor, there is hardly any doubt that these problems will soon be minimized.

THE EVOLUTION OF GHANA LAW SINCE INDEPENDENCE

WILLIAM BURNETT HARVEY*

INTRODUCTION

On March 6, 1957, the British Gold Coast achieved independence in circumstances that apparently offered a bright future for sovereign, independent Ghana. Since 1951, adroit leaders of a well-organized political party had operated a responsible parliamentary government under British tutelage and reservations of power that was in fact never exercised. A growing body of African civil servants was supplemented at critical points by expatriate officers whose continued work in Ghana was assured by attractive economic arrangements. The national economy was prosperous, there was no encumbering debt, and the young government could plan national development fortified by large foreign exchange reserves. Independence was celebrated under a warm aura of goodwill toward the former colonial masters who in turn regarded the infant state as the vindication of decades of colonial administration in sub-Saharan Africa.

Since 1957, numerous other areas in Africa have achieved independence, but for many reasons Ghana has kept its position in the limelight. Its domestic problems, great and small, have occupied the world press which, unfortunately, has not always coupled its freedom to report with responsibility. On the international scene, Ghanaian activism has from time to time touched raw Cold War nerve ends, and Ghana like many of the new countries has felt the need of constant vigil to avoid becoming a mere pawn in the great East-West struggle.

Much of Ghana's post-independence development is of great interest, but this paper is limited to the evolution of its legal order. Before turning to the central subject, the hierarchy of norms comprising the law of Ghana, it will be helpful to sketch briefly the main course of constitutional development, emphasizing those aspects which relate most directly to the legal order in the narrower sense. Thus the legislative and executive establishments will be surveyed briefly, while the courts system will be described in somewhat greater detail. Since the functioning of any legal order is materially influenced by the professional lawyers, mention must also be made of the character and role of the bar.

I

CONSTITUTIONAL STRUCTURE

A. The Legislative Branch

On the granting of independence the legislative power of Ghana was vested in a Parliament of 104 members, 72 of whom were supporters of Dr. Kwame Nkrumah's

---

* A.B. 1943, Wake Forest College; J.D. 1949, University of Michigan; Post Doctoral Fellow, University of Heidelberg, 1955-56. Professor of Law, University of Michigan. Dean of the Law Faculty, University of Ghana, and Director of Legal Education of Ghana.

Convention People's Party. In general the institutional forms of the British parliamentary system were adopted. The written Constitution,[1] however, imposed three substantive limitations on the legislative power of Parliament: (1) No law could "make persons of any racial community liable to disabilities to which persons of other such communities are not made liable."[2] (2) Except for restrictions imposed for the preservation of public order, morality, or health, no law could "deprive any person of his freedom of conscience or the right freely to profess, practice or propagate any religion."[3] (3) The taking of private property was subject to a right of adequate compensation, the amount to be judicially determined.[4] In addition, the Constitution established certain procedural limitations on the exercise of legislative power, some involving the necessity for approval by regional organs. These special procedures applied to Acts altering regional boundaries and names of regions,[5] affecting the status and functions of chiefs,[6] or modifying the constitutional provisions of Ghana.[7] The various limitations, both substantive and procedural, were supported by a power of judicial review of legislation granted to the Supreme Court.[8] The National Assembly, which was required to meet at least once a year,[9] had a maximum life of five years.[10]

Between the Independence Constitution of 1957 and the Republican Constitution of 1960, the most significant constitutional change affecting the legislative establishment was the repeal in 1958 of the provisions requiring special procedures for Acts revising the Constitution, altering regional boundaries, or affecting the chiefs.[11] The three substantive limitations remained, but the National Assembly thus moved significantly toward full legislative sovereignty.

Following a national plebiscite in April 1960, when a tentative draft constitution was placed before the electorate, the Republic of Ghana came into existence on July 1, 1960. The Republican Constitution articulates a theory of popular sovereignty[12] which is directly reflected in the entrenchment of a number of provisions of the Constitution; entrenchment insulates them against change except after popular approval in a referendum ordered by the President.[13] Aside from this entrenchment device, the legislative powers of Parliament are not limited.[14] The three substantive safeguards of the 1957 Constitution survived only in a diluted form as part of a "solemn declaration before the people" which the President is required to make immediately after assuming office.[15] The ultimate legislative competence of the

---

[1] The Independence Constitution was promulgated as an Order in Council. [1957] 1 STAT. INSTR. 1036 (No. 277).
[2] *Id.* § 31(2).   [3] *Id.* § 31(3).   [4] *Id.* § 34.
[5] *Id.* § 33.   [6] *Id.* §§ 32(2)(3), 66-68.   [7] *Id.* § 32.
[8] *Id.* § 31(5).   [9] *Id.* § 46.   [10] *Id.* § 47(2).
[11] The Constitution (Repeal of Restrictions) Act, No. 38 of 1958.
[12] REPUBLICAN CONST. art. I.   [13] *Id.* art. 20(2) and (4).   [14] *Id.* art. 20(6).
[15] *Id.* art. 13. The argument that the presidential declaration required by art. 13(1) of the Constitution has juridical effect as a constitutional Bill of Rights limiting the legislative power of Parliament was rejected by the Supreme Court of Ghana in the *Baffour Osei Akoto* case, Civ. Appeal No. 42/61, Aug. 28, 1961. Chief Justice Korsah, for the Court, said that the provisions of article 13(1) "are, in our view, similar to the Coronation Oath taken by the Queen of England during the Coronation Service. In the

Assembly is curtailed, however, by the necessity for presidential assent before a bill can become effective,[16] by the prohibition of amendments of the annual estimates (money bills) submitted by the Cabinet,[17] and is at least qualified by the special legislative powers of the first President[18] which will be mentioned later.

B. The Executive

In the conventional language of British constitutional law, the 1957 Independence Constitution vested executive power in the Queen, to "be exercised by the Queen or by the Governor-General as Her representative."[19] The appointment of the Governor-General[20] and the exercise of his powers were subject to the constitutional conventions applicable in the United Kingdom to the powers and functions of the Queen.[21] Thus the executive power was actually wielded by a Cabinet headed by Dr. Nkrumah, responsible to the National Assembly. In general British practices were adopted; however, the constitutional document itself included a good bit of detail and in a few situations departed from the British model.[22] This structure of the Executive was preserved until the advent of the Republic in 1960.

The Republican Constitution conferred executive power on the President who is the Head of the State and Commander-in-Chief of the Armed Forces. The President is declared to be responsible to the people.[23] He is to be elected[24] by the National Assembly acting as an electoral college, but the first presidential vote in the Assembly is automatically cast on the basis of preferences declared by members of the Assembly prior to their election. If no candidate receives a majority on the first ballot, members of the Assembly may vote their uncommitted preferences on subsequent ballots. If a President has not been elected on the completion of five ballots, the Assembly is deemed dissolved and new elections must be held with parliamentary candidates again declaring a binding presidential preference.

On election the President appoints his Cabinet who must be Members of Parliament though they are not responsible to Parliament.[25] The President may at any

---

one case the President is required to make a solemn declaration, in the other the Queen is required to take a solemn oath. Neither the oath nor the declaration can be said to have a statutory effect of an enactment of Parliament. The suggestion that the declarations made by the President or assumption of office constitute a 'Bill of Rights' in the sense in which the expression is understood under the Constitution of the United States of America is therefore untenable."

[16] REPUBLICAN CONST. art. 24.   [17] *Id.* art. 31(2).   [18] *Id.* art. 55.

[19] The Ghana (Constitution) Order in Council, [1957] 1 STAT. INSTR. 1036 (No. 277), § 6.

[20] The 1957 Constitution, § 4(1), merely vested the appointing power in the Queen. The British Government expressly recognized, however, that the Governor-General was to be appointed "in accordance with the conventions obtaining in other Commonwealth countries." *The Proposed Constitution of Ghana,* CMND. No. 71, at 4 (1957). The convention contemplated appointment on the advice of the Ghana Government. See also 5 HALSBURY'S LAWS OF ENGLAND 448 (3d ed. 1953).

[21] The Ghana (Constitution) Order in Council, [1957] 1 STAT. INSTR. 1036 (No. 277), § 4.

[22] For example, § 8(1) of the Constitution provided that the offices of the Ministers should become vacant whenever the office of Prime Minister became vacant and a new Prime Minister had been appointed.

[23] REPUBLICAN CONST. art. 8.

[24] Relevant provisions on the election of the President appear in article 11 of the Republican Constitution and in the Presidential Elections Act, Act. No. 1 of 1960.

[25] REPUBLICAN CONST. arts. 15, 16.

time dissolve the Assembly.[26] Thus if there should arise between the President and the Assembly differences of a kind that in a parliamentary system might produce a vote of no confidence or the breakdown of a really viable cooperation, the President is able to permit the people at any time to resolve the issues in a new general election. It should be noted, however, that restraint in dissolving the Assembly may be recommended by the fact that on dissolution a new presidential election must also be held, the President's term depending directly on the life of the Assembly. Should the President decline to dissolve the Assembly, no breakdown of cooperation, even to the extent of a direct expression of lack of confidence in the Executive, can force the President out of office. This fact may take on added significance in view of the special legislative powers of the first President, to be noted later.

Dr. Nkrumah was declared first President of Ghana.[27] He was not elected by the processes described above but by a plebiscite conducted at the time the draft Republican Constitution was submitted to the people. In addition to the variety of executive powers conferred by the Constitution on any President, Dr. Nkrumah as first President was granted during his initial period in office the power to "give directions by legislative instrument."[28] The "initial period in office" is defined to mean "until some other person assumes office as President." Since an incumbent President is eligible for re-election any number of times,[29] Dr. Nkrumah will enjoy the same legislative powers in any terms for which he is elected to succeed himself. Thus far, these special legislative powers of the President do not appear to have been exercised.

C. The Court System

A cardinal feature of the judicial order of Ghana, continued from its colonial past, is the division of judicial power between two systems of courts, one administering customary law of the bulk of the African population and the other applying British law or the recently developed national law to a much smaller European and African population. The evolution of both systems will be traced briefly. It should also be observed preliminarily that the judicial order has never appeared as a major point of controversy in the course of Ghana's constitutional evolution; post-independence developments have thus been able to proceed quietly, largely along lines projected from the colonial period.

At the date of independence, systems of Native Courts existed under separate legislation for the Colony,[30] Ashanti,[31] the Northern Territories,[32] and Togoland[33]

---

[26] *Id.* art. 23(1).   [27] *Id.* art. 10.   [28] *Id.* art. 55.
[29] *Id.* art. 11; Presidential Elections Act, Act No. 1 of 1960, §§ 4-5.
[30] Native Courts (Colony) Ordinance, No. 22 of 1944, as amended, CAP. 98, LAWS OF THE GOLD COAST (1951).
[31] Native Courts (Ashanti) Ordinance, No. 2 of 1935, as amended, CAP. 99, LAWS OF THE GOLD COAST (1951).
[32] Native Courts (North Territories) Ordinance, No. 31 of 1935, as amended, CAP. 104, LAWS OF THE GOLD COAST (1951).
[33] Native Courts (Southern Section of Togoland) Ordinance, No. 8 of 1949, CAP. 106, LAWS OF THE GOLD COAST (1951).

which together formed modern Ghana. Numerous relatively minor differences among the several systems will be ignored in this survey. The establishment of a Native Court and the authority of its members to sit depended upon the order of the colonial Governor and not upon chiefly status in the indigenous society. Such courts were, however, largely staffed by the chiefs and their counsellors. No special qualifications were demanded for appointment to a Court, but it was generally assumed that the members would be familiar with native law and custom in their own areas.

The jurisdiction of the Native Courts was defined in terms of both persons and subject matter. In general it may be said that jurisdiction over persons followed ethnic lines, including "persons of African descent" or "natives." It was possible for non-Africans to come within the jurisdiction of the Native Courts by voluntary submission or official direction, as well as for Africans to leave the jurisdiction by not following the "mode of life . . . of the general community" or on a transactional basis by agreeing that British law should apply. Jurisdiction over subject matter was limited to civil claims under native customary law, certain customary offenses, causes arising under a few Ordinances and minor offenses under the Criminal Code. The Native Courts systems were related to the higher judicial order and the colonial administration by three basic control devices: (1) appeals to higher tribunals within the Native Courts system and in limited instances to an appeal tribunal outside the system; (2) transfers of cases from one Native Court to another or to a Magistrate's Court; and (3) review and revision of court action by District Commissioners or the Judicial Adviser. Professional lawyers were not permitted to practice before the Native Courts, but the charge was officially made that a group of "bush lawyers" actively practiced.[34]

The existing systems of Native Courts were unaffected by the grant of independence in 1957. A major attempt to revise the systems was made, however, in the Local Courts Act of 1958.[35] The objective of the Act was a nationally uniform system of Local Courts without the hierarchy of grades formerly used. The substantive jurisdiction of the new courts was to be that of former Grade A Native Courts over minor civil cases and petty crimes, and the enforcement of a few Ordinances. An effort was made to eliminate the racial criterion for jurisdiction over persons which had applied in Native Courts. The change was largely formal, however, since the substantive jurisdiction continued to depend in the main on the application of customary law. The new Act also reflects an effort to maintain a higher quality of operation in the Local Courts through standards of efficiency for appointment as a court officer, courses of instruction, national supervision of arrangements of local government authorities for the courts, and the periodic inspection of court records.[36] Administrative control over court operations was reduced, but control by

[34] NATIVE TRIBUNALS COMMITTEE OF ENQUIRY, REPORT 14 (Accra, 1943).
[35] The Local Courts Act, Act No. 23 of 1958.
[36] The Local Courts Act did not contemplate the immediate disestablishment of all Native Courts but rather their gradual replacement by Local Courts as personnel and facilities become available. The first Local Courts were not established until December 1959 when 23 Local Courts Magistrates were appointed

appeals and transfers of causes continued to be exercised. The Local Courts system as described was preserved by the Courts Act of 1960[37] which became effective on the advent of the Republic.

The higher judicial structure revised at the time of independence consisted of a Supreme Court, composed of the High Court of Justice and the Court of Appeal,[38] and at the local level a system of Magistrates' Courts.[39] The High Court of Justice was granted a wide range of original jurisdiction in major matters as well as appellate jurisdiction from Magistrates' Courts.[40] The Court of Appeal was granted appellate powers in important cases from all lower courts, including Native Courts.[41] It thus assumed jurisdiction over Gold Coast cases formerly enjoyed by the West African Court of Appeals, and appeal to that Court was abolished.[42] Appeal from the Supreme Court of Ghana to the Judicial Committee of the Privy Council was retained[43] until the advent of the Republic in 1960.[44] The tenure of Supreme Court Judges was protected by a constitutional provision for removal only on the address of the Assembly carried by not less than two-thirds of the membership, asking removal on the ground of stated misbehavior or infirmity of body or mind,[45] and by a guarantee against diminution of salary during a judge's term of office.[46] No such safeguards were provided, however, for judicial officers below the Supreme Court.

The Republican Constitution conferred the judicial power of Ghana on a Supreme Court and a High Court, designated the superior courts, and such inferior courts as might be created by law.[47] The Courts Act of 1960[48] contained very little innovation in its elaboration of the judicial structure. The Act was a consolidation of existing legislation with some modification of detail. Court names were somewhat changed, and a new system of Circuit Courts was introduced between the High Court and the District Courts.[49] The power to appoint judges and judicial officers was somewhat more firmly concentrated in the President.[50] The former safeguards

---

in the Eastern Region. On June 24, 1960, the remainder of the Native Courts were disestablished; 114 Local Courts Magistrates have been appointed, replacing about 170 former Native Courts. Thus far relatively little progress has been made in establishing training programs for Magistrates and other court officers, though Mr. John Jackson, the Senior Local Courts Adviser, is pressing efforts toward that end.

[37] Courts Act, 1960, C. A. 9. All enactments of the Constituent Assembly are separately numbered.
[38] The Courts (Amendment) Ordinance, No. 17 of 1957, § 2.
[39] Courts Ordinance, No. 7 of 1935, as amended, CAP. 4, LAWS OF THE GOLD COAST (1951).
[40] The Courts (Amendment) Ordinance, No. 17 of 1957, § 9.
[41] The Court of Appeal Ordinance, No. 35 of 1957.
[42] Id. § 23.
[43] The Ghana (Appeal to Privy Council) Order in Council, [1957] 1 STAT. INSTR. 1197 (No. 1361).
[44] REPUBLICAN CONST. art. 42(1). By agreement between the Government of the United Kingdom and the Government of Ghana, appeals registered in the Privy Council office before the date on which Ghana became a Republic would be heard. *Exchange of Letters,* CMND. NO. 1190 (1960).
[45] The Ghana (Constitution) Order in Council, [1957] 1 STAT. INSTR. 1036 (No. 277), § 54(3).
[46] Id. § 54(7).
[47] REPUBLICAN CONST. art. 41.
[48] Courts Act, 1960, C. A. 9.
[49] By Legislative Instrument 45 of 1960, the Chief Justice divided the country into seven circuits, each circuit being composed of one of the Regions as defined in the Regions of Ghana Act, 1960, C. A. 11, except that the Northern and Upper Regions were combined into one circuit.
[50] REPUBLICAN CONST. art. 45(1); Judicial Service Act, 1960, C. A. 10, § 7.

of tenure and salary were preserved for judges of the Supreme Court and High Court but were not extended further through the judicial system.[51]

D. The Bar

In its resources of legal talent Ghana is more fortunate than many of the new African states. Precise figures are not available, but it appears that about 350 lawyers are now authorized to practice in Ghana. Virtually all were qualified in England as barristers or solicitors, but recently a program for local qualification has been instituted.[52] Lawyers at the Ghana bar may practice as both barrister and solicitor, though certain requirements of practical training are imposed for a license to practice in the latter capacity.[53]

II

THE HIERARCHY OF LEGAL NORMS

The legal order in Ghana is pluralistic, encompassing not merely law derived from the former colonial power, now supplemented by post-independence legislation, and a system of courts to apply that law, but also a body of indigenous or customary law applied mainly in the Native, now Local, Courts. To avoid chaos some scheme was necessary to delimit the sphere of operation of each body of law and each system of courts and, in so far as these spheres coincided or conflicted, to determine which should prevail.

A. Horizontal and Vertical Ordering

Two basic methods for interrelating the component elements in a pluralistic system may be distinguished. The first involves the definition of discrete substantive areas of operation for each element in the system, with each element entirely uncontrolled by the other so long as it remains within its assigned area. Thus, for example, it is conceivable that the definition of major crimes such as murder, rape, and robbery might be made the function of English law or a nationally legislated norm and the application of that law assigned to a system of superior courts, while all other interpersonal relations of which the law took account were left entirely to a body or bodies of customary law applied in courts established by the indigenous regimes. Such a division of function between two systems may be referred to as involving horizontal ordering.

The other type of order is hierarchical or vertical. In this type the bodies of law and the applying courts are related as superiors and inferiors. While hierarchical ordering may permit some horizontal division of functions at least in the early stages of law application, it allows ultimate resort to the higher courts applying the superior or ultimately governing body of law in an appeal or some other type of supervisory proceeding. While such a distinction of types of relations is useful for

[51] REPUBLICAN CONST. arts. 45(3), 46(1).
[52] Legal Profession Act, Act 32 of 1960, §§ 13-15.
[53] *Id.* §§ 2, 8.

some analyses,[54] it would appear that in every pluralistic system there is an irreducible minimum of hierarchical or vertical ordering, since some overriding set of norms must at least define authoritatively the spheres of operation and application of the several bodies of law.

B. The Courts Ordinance, 1935

The general standards defining the relations between English-derived law and native customary law in the pre-independence Gold Coast were found in the Courts Ordinance.[55] It bears emphasis that these general standards were posited by the imperial power. Thus any ordering of the relations of English and indigenous law of the horizontal variety fitted into an overall hierarchical pattern dominated by imperial law. Both horizontal and hierarchical ordering were used, however, within that general structure.

The Courts Ordinance, section eighty-three, provided that "subject to the terms of this or any other Ordinance, the common law, the doctrines of equity, and the statutes of general application which were in force in England on the 24th day of July, 1874, shall be in force within the jurisdiction of the Courts." The specified date derived its significance from the fact that the Gold Coast then acquired a local Legislature. English law made applicable in the Gold Coast by this section consisted of four elements: (1) local ordinances, (2) common law, (3) doctrines of equity, and (4) statutes of general application in force in England on the cut-off date. It is entirely clear, of course, that English statutes of general application that came into force after July 24, 1874, were not *per se* applicable to the Gold Coast.

The question may be raised whether the same cut-off date applied to the common law and doctrines of equity, so that norms from these sources were applicable in the Gold Coast only as developed and articulated up to the cut-off date. The language of section eighty-three and the punctuation suggest that the cut-off date applies only to statutes of general application, thus making common law and equity doctrines as developed later by English courts also part of the Gold Coast law. Unless, however, one assumes an eternal completeness and immutability of common law and equity, these being merely discovered but not created by the courts, the same rationale underlying a cut-off date for statutes of general application would appear applicable to common law and equity as well.

Current acceptance of the view that courts do create law in the decision of cases on a common law or equity basis therefore suggests that English developments in these spheres after July 24, 1874, were not applicable in the Gold Coast. This conclusion finds some support in section seventeen of the Courts Ordinance which provided that the Supreme Court of the Gold Coast should exercise its jurisdiction in probate, divorce, and matrimonial matters "in conformity with the law and

---

[54] For a useful application of this distinction to the international order, see Falk, *International Jurisdiction: Horizontal and Vertical Conceptions of Legal Order*, 32 TEMP. L.Q. 295 (1959).

[55] Courts Ordinance, No. 7 of 1935 as amended, CAP. 4, LAWS OF THE GOLD COAST (1951), §§ 83-89.

practice for the time being in force in England." Evidently the draftsmen of the Ordinance were entirely competent to find language appropriate to an intention that the law in the Gold Coast should be continuously related to the current state of the law in England. It is thus arguable that the cut-off date in section eighty-three applied not only to statutes of general application but to common law and equity as well. This question was never authoritatively settled, however, while the Courts Ordinance remained in force.[56]

A further contribution of English law to the legal order of the Gold Coast consisted of "imperial laws declared to extend or apply to the jurisdiction of the Courts" (section eighty-five). Such laws were to apply only within the limits of local jurisdiction and to the extent local circumstances permitted. These relatively vague criteria necessitated more precise definition by judicial decision of the applicability of imperial laws. Similarly, courts in the Gold Coast were authorized to construe imperial laws with such alterations not affecting the substance of the enactment as would facilitate their application.

To handle cases of conflict among the norms derived from English law, a distinct hierarchy was required. Clearly, the paramount norms were those provided by imperial laws made expressly applicable to the Gold Coast or extended thereto by Orders in Council. Next in a descending order were those norms provided by local Gold Coast legislation. English statutes of general application in force in 1874 were received in the Gold Coast as legislation. Prevailing ideas of legislative supremacy would, of course, cause these statutes to prevail in cases of conflict with common law or equity doctrines. In the final cases of conflict between law and equity, which were concurrently administered in the superior courts of the Gold Coast, the rules of equity were to prevail (section eighty-six).

This hierarchical order of English norms co-existed with a number of bodies of customary law[57] in force in various parts of the Gold Coast. Standards determining the relation of customary law to English law in a horizontal order were provided by section eighty-seven of the Courts Ordinance. Primarily these standards were ethnic. In causes or matters the parties to which were "natives," the primary law presumptively applicable was customary law. A party could, however, lose the benefit of customary law if it appeared either from an express contract or from

---

[56] The best available analysis of this problem and the related question of the extent to which English decisions were binding on Gold Coast Courts is Allott, *The Authority of English Decisions in Colonial Courts*, 1 J. AFRICAN LAW 23 (1957).

[57] The Courts Ordinance did not use the "customary law." It spoke rather of "native law or custom" and "local law or custom." Neither of these terms, which do not seem to differ in substantive meaning, was defined in the Ordinance. However, the Native Courts (Colony) Ordinance, No. 22 of 1944 as amended, CAP. 98, LAWS OF THE GOLD COAST (1951), § 2, defines "native customary law" as "a rule or body of rules regulating rights and imposing correlative duties, being a rule or body of rules which obtains and is fortified by established native usage and which is appropriate and applicable to any particular cause, action, suit, matter, dispute, issue or question, and includes also any native customary law recorded or modified in accordance with the provisions of sections 30 and 31 respectively of the Native Authority (Colony) Ordinance, 1944." The procedure for the declaration or modification of customary laws by the traditional authorities will be discussed later.

the nature of the transaction out of which the question arose that the party had agreed to have his obligations regulated exclusively by English law. If the parties to the cause or transaction included both natives and non-natives, English law was presumably controlling. Even in such a case, however, the courts were authorized to apply customary law if they determined that "substantial injustice would be done to either party by a strict adherence to the rules of English law."

Overriding this horizontal relation of English and customary law based on ethnic criteria was a hierarchical relation of customary law to certain limiting principles. Not all native law and custom existing in the Gold Coast was retained, but only such as was not "repugnant to natural justice, equity and good conscience" and not "incompatible either directly or by necessary implication with any ordinance for the time being in force."[58] Determinations of repugnancy or incompatibility were to be made by the courts.

In the main, the courts which actually invoked these limiting criteria were the superior courts, staffed principally by English personnel, though it was possible for a Native Court to exclude customary law on such grounds.[59] Clearly in the case of incompatibility with any Ordinance, the standard invalidating the customary law was supplied by the colonial power. The "brooding omnipresence" of English law was further strengthened by the overriding standards of "natural justice, equity and good conscience" which impliedly were incorporated in English law or were at least revealed to the eyes of English judges. The same basis for decision was provided for any case within the jurisdiction of the Native Courts to which no express rule of the customary law was applicable.[60]

This pluralistic system created an appalling number of problems, most of which were neither clearly nor satisfactorily solved prior to the repeal of the Courts Ordinance. These difficulties need only be touched upon here. A serious issue was posed by the doctrine of precedent or stare decisis whereby the decisions of higher courts are binding on lower courts in the hierarchy. In applying this doctrine much uncertainty existed as to the binding effect on Gold Coast courts of decisions of the English High Court, the Court of Criminal Appeals, and the House of Lords.[61] We have already noted the question whether the cut-off date in section eighty-three of the Courts Ordinance applied to common law and equity as well as to English statutes of general application. There were also difficulties related to the

[58] Courts Ordinance, *supra* note 57, at § 87(1).

[59] Matson, *Internal Conflicts of Laws in the Gold Coast*, 16 MODERN L. REV. 469 (1953), indicates that the repugnancy standard has been used occasionally to deal with procedural irregularities in native courts, but that the two principal categories of repugnancy cases are those involving slavery or practices analogized to slavery and cases involving disturbance of long-continued, bona fide possession of land.

[60] See Matson, *supra* note 59, at 475-76, for the suggestion that in certain types of cases between natives, for example those involving the use of abusive or derogatory remarks, the courts have applied the English law of torts with "no pretence that that law is the embodiment of 'justice, equity and good conscience,' applied in the absence of any 'express rule' of customary law; they [the courts] do not consider the possibility that such a rule may exist."

[61] On this problem see Allott, *supra* note 56; Elias, *Colonial Courts and the Doctrine of Judicial Precedent*, 18 MODERN L. REV. 356 (1955).

reception of such statutes themselves. What statutes fell within this category? Might parts of a statute be "of general application" and thus be applicable though other parts clearly were not? As a purely practical matter, how easily could a lawyer in the Gold Coast discover the English statutes in force in 1874?[62]

The problems created by the application of customary law were probably even more difficult. Standards for solving the perplexing problem of excluding customary law in causes between natives on the basis of express or implied agreement that English law should govern were never adequately set out by the courts. When was such an agreement to be implied?[63] When not all parties were natives, in what circumstances would the court's perception of injustice to one of the parties foreclose the application of English law and warrant resort to native law and custom?[64]

Perhaps most difficult of all was the matter of ascertaining the customary law in situations where the general hierarchy of norms indicated its applicability. The Courts Ordinance, section 87(2), provided that a court might "give effect to any book or manuscript recognized in the Gold Coast as a legal authority" and might "call to its assistance chiefs or other persons whom the Court considers to have special knowledge of native law and custom." The courts were also authorized (section eighty-nine) to refer questions of native law and custom to a competent Native Court for determination. Decisions of Native Courts on such referred questions were not appealable, but the referring court was in no way bound by them. The courts could accept or reject them, in whole or in part.

The methods for ascertaining customary law were entirely different in the superior or English courts and in the Native Courts. In the latter, customary law was assumed to be known to the members of the court who could apply it on the basis of their own knowledge, although a party relying on a particular custom was free to call witnesses to prove it.[65] In the British courts, however, magistrates and judges could not be presumed to be familiar with the indigenous customary law; indeed, they were foreclosed from relying on such personal knowledge as their prior experience might provide. The party relying on customary law was therefore required to lay an adequate basis by allegation and proof for the court's application of customary law. The West African Court of Appeal held that "where a party intends to set up and rely upon a Native Law and Custom it must be specifically alleged and pleaded."[66] This requirement was confirmed by court rules necessitating the pleading not merely of the substantive effect of the native law or custom but also the geographic area and the tribe or tribes to which it related.[67]

[62] See Atiyah, *Commercial Law in Ghana*, 1960 J. BUSINESS LAW 430.
[63] For examples of judicial treatment of this problem, see Kwesi-Johnston v. Effie, 14 W.A.C.A. 254 (1953) and Ferguson v. Duncan, 14 W.A.C.A. 316 (1953).
[64] For cases in point see Koney v. Union Trading Co., Ltd., 2 W.A.C.A. 188 (1934); Nelson & anor. v. Nelson & othr., 13 W.A.C.A. 248 (1951).
[65] Ababio II v. Nsemfoo, 12 W.A.C.A. 127 (1947).
[66] Bonsi v. Adjena II, 6 W.A.C.A. 241 (1940).
[67] Supreme Court (Civil Procedure) Rules, Ord. 19, r 31

Once adequate pleading opened the door, proof of the customary law itself remained difficult. By dictum in *Angu v. Attah,* the Privy Council declared that customary law "has to be proved in the first instance by calling witnesses acquainted with the native customs until the particular customs have, by frequent proof in the Courts, become so notorious that the Courts take judicial notice of them."[68] The evidence contemplated by the first branch of this rule might come from chiefs, linguists, or others who could be qualified as experts on customary law. As mentioned earlier, the Courts Ordinance also permitted proof of customary law by the use of "any book or manuscript recognized in the Gold Coast as a legal authority" (section 87(2)), and by reports from Native Courts on questions referred to them (section eighty-nine).

Incidentally it may be noted that use of textbooks or documents for the proof of customary law high-lighted a further complication. Such law was not uniform throughout the Gold Coast; on the contrary major differences existed between the principal cultural or tribal groups, and even within the same groups local variations were always a possibility. Thus even after a decision was reached that a cause was governed by customary law, the internal choice of law remained. Yet these complex problems were often overlooked by the courts. Particularly was this the case when customary law was proved by the use of textbooks. The most prominent of such works in the Gold Coast were the works of John M. Sarbah on Fanti law.[69] The Fantis are a branch of the larger Akan group and are concentrated in the southwestern areas of the country. Sarbah had declared that "Fanti laws and customs apply to all Akans and Fantis, and to all persons whose mothers are of Akan or Fanti race."[70] This seems a most doubtful generalization when one considers that the Ashanti are also Akans. Even the author made no pretension, however, that he described the laws of the Ga-Adangbe, Ewe, or other non-Akan peoples of the Gold Coast. Yet not infrequently the British courts accepted Sarbah's work as indicative of the applicable customary law between non-Fanti and even non-Akan parties.[71]

Determination of customary law as fact by the introduction of evidence is inconvenient and time-consuming as well as productive of uncertainty. The second branch of the dictum of *Angu v. Attah* suggested the possibility of dispensing with evidence when "the particular customs have, by frequent proof in the Courts, become so notorious that the Courts take judicial notice of them." Yet twenty-one years later, the Privy Council observed that "their Lordships have not been informed of any customary law so established; and they may observe that it would be very convenient if the Courts in West Africa in suitable cases would rule as to the native

---

[68] (1915) Gold Coast Privy Council Judgments, 1874-1928, at 43, 44. This dictum was later approved by the Judicial Committee in Amissah v. Krabah, 2 W.A.C.A. 30 (1936).
[69] JOHN M. SARBAH, FANTI CUSTOMARY LAWS 16 (1897); JOHN M. SARBAH, FANTI LAW REPORT (1904).
[70] JOHN M. SARBAH, FANTI CUSTOMARY LAWS 16 (1897).
[71] See Matson, *supra* note 59, at 478-81, for a review of relevant cases.

customs of which they think it proper to take judicial notice, specifying, of course, the tribes (or districts) concerned and taking steps to see that these rulings are reported in a readily accessible form."[72]

While this method of establishing the content of the customary law has the advantages of convenience and certainty, it could also have the disadvantage of freezing the development of customary law, separating it from the on-going life of the community and in fact entirely changing the basis of its obligatory quality. In general, customary law is deemed binding because it reflects the consensus of the community as reflected in actual usage. When the custom becomes subject to judicial notice, however, it arguably derives its force not from usage but from the acceptance and implementation by the courts. If, as has been suggested,[73] it was open to a party to show even after judicial recognition that a custom was no longer supported by established usage, much of the advantage of convenience and certainty attributable to judicial notice of oft-proved customary law would be lost. The admission of such proof would mean that judicial recognition of a custom had done little more than shift the burden of proof in a lawsuit.

Another device for establishing customary law without proof of usage was provided by legislation authorizing certain traditional authorities to make declarations of customary law or recommend its modification. An example of such legislation was the Native Law and Custom (Ashanti Confederacy Council) Ordinance of 1940,[74] which authorized the Confederacy Council to declare what in its opinion was the native law and custom within the Confederacy relating to any subject. If the Governor in Council was satisfied that the declaration truly recorded the custom and was not repugnant to justice, equity or good conscience or incompatible with any Ordinance, he might declare it to be in force with the result that every court would be required to accept it as determinative of the customary law on the specified subject. The same Ordinance authorized the Confederacy Council to recommend modifications of native law and custom, which, subject to the same criteria, the Governor in Council might accept and implement.[75] These powers have been negligibly used by the traditional authorities. It appears clear, however, that in so far as they are used, the law so declared ceases in fact to be customary

---

[72] Amissah v. Krabah, 2 W.A.C.A. 30, 31 (1936).

[73] Allott, *The Judicial Ascertainment of Customary Law in British Africa*, 20 MODERN L. REV. 244 (1957).

[74] Native Law and Custom (Ashanti Confederacy Council) Ordinance, No. 4 of 1940, CAP. 102, LAWS OF THE GOLD COAST (1951).

[75] Similar legislation for other divisions of the Gold Coast is the State Councils (Northern Territories) Ordinance, No. 4 of 1952, §§ 12, 13; the State Councils (Colony and Southern Togoland) Ordinance, No. 8 of 1952, §§ 13, 14. The post-independence Houses of Chiefs Act, Act No. 20 of 1958, § 16(1), authorized a House of Chiefs to submit to the Governor-General or to the Speaker of the Assembly "a written declaration of what in its opinion is the customary law relating to any subject in force in any part of the area of its authority." The Act was silent, however, as to the status such a declaration would have in the courts or the functions it would perform for the legislative or executive branch.

law and becomes a form of legislation, deriving its force like any positive law from being authoritatively laid down by official agencies.[76]

This brief sketch by no means exhausts the problems presented in administering the pluralistic legal order of the Gold Coast. Our purpose has been only to outline the various sources and kinds of legal norms and to indicate their relations in a general hierarchical and horizontal structure. It remains to consider the extent to which that structure has been modified in the post-independence legal order of Ghana, and to look briefly at the contribution which the changes may have made toward solution of the practical problems of administering justice.

C. The Post-Independence Legal Order

The hierarchy of legal norms was not greatly affected by the grant of independence on March 6, 1957. After that date, of course, the supreme position in the hierarchy was occupied by the constitutional Order in Council. Next came local legislation in the form of Acts of Parliament. No British statute enacted after independence extended to Ghana unless the Parliament of Ghana requested and consented to the enactment. Otherwise the pre-independence body of law was left intact.[77] This basis structure of legal norms remained until the advent of the Republic on July 1, 1960, when the Republican Constitution and certain Acts of the Constituent Assembly made significant changes.

The basic statement on the new order of legal norms in Ghana is found in the Constitution, article forty, which provides:

Except as may be otherwise provided by an enactment made after the coming into operation of the Constitution, the laws of Ghana comprise the following—
   (a) the Constitution,
   (b) enactments made by or under the authority of the Parliament established by the Constitution,
   (c) enactments other than the Constitution made by or under the authority of the Constituent Assembly,
   (d) enactments in force immediately before the coming into operation of the Constitution,
   (e) the common law, and
   (f) customary law.

The constitutional list is suggestive of a hierarchical ordering but this is not made clear in the Constitution itself. For clarification of the new structure of norms we must turn to two enactments of the Constituent Assembly—the Interpretation Act[78] and the Courts Act.[79]

The Interpretation Act of 1960 (section 17(1)) provides that the common law received as part of the laws of Ghana includes, in addition to the rules generally known as the common law, the doctrines of equity and "rules of customary law included in

---
[76] For a full discussion of these problems see Allott, *supra* note 73.
[77] Ghana Independence Act, 1957, 5 & 6 Eliz. 2, c. 6, § 1.
[78] Interpretation Act, 1960, C.A. 4.
[79] Courts Act, 1960, C.A. 9.

the common law under any enactment providing for the assimilation of such rules of customary law as are suitable for general application." The effect of this provision for assimilation is not yet clear. A Ghanaian scholar has suggested that the assimilation device may "have been the sugar-coating which served to enable the drafters or their instructors to administer the common law pill to Ghana's lawmakers." The same author continues:

> Short of legislative enactment by the national legislature, it is not easy to see how it can be left to the courts to decide which customary law rules to assimilate and generalize, and how communities subject to a different system of customary law of which they are equally proud are going to be induced to drop their own rule merely because the court has seen fit, in some particular case before it, to declare that a particular rule of customary law in one system is suitable for universal application and should be assimilated into the common law. This would seem to indicate that it would be preferable for the national legislature rather than the courts to tackle the general problem of customary law.[80]

It must be observed, however, that the Interpretation Act contemplated legislation on the subject of assimilation of customary law.

Basic implementing provisions were incorporated in the Chieftaincy Act of 1961. This statute commits the task of assimilating customary law into the common law not to the courts but to the Chiefs, the traditional rulers, subject to the ultimate discretion of the executive. On the initiative of either a Regional House of Chiefs or the Minister of Local Government, a joint committee drawn from the Houses of Chiefs of all the Regions may be convened to consider whether a customary law rule should be assimilated by the common law. If the joint committee favors assimilation, they may draft a declaration "with such modifications as they may consider desirable" for submission to the Minister.[81] After consulting the Chief Justice, if the Minister is satisfied that effect should be given to the draft "either as submitted or with such modifications as he considers necessary," he may effect the assimilation by a legislative instrument.[82] The resulting common law rule of customary origin has priority of application within its scope over other rules derived from the common law or any system of customary law.[83] The Minister has discretion to devise transitional provisions relating to cases pending when the assimilation instrument is made.[84]

It is noteworthy that this assimilation scheme sanctions consciously legislative adjustments in the customary and common law. The Chiefs may recommend assimilation of an existing customary law rule or some modification. The Minister may decree the assimilation of the rule recommended by the Chiefs or modify it as he thinks necessary. Thus significant powers for effecting legal change are lodged in persons outside the conventional legislative and judicial structure. It does not appear, however, that these powers have been exercised up to this time.

[80] Bensi-Enchill, *Ghana Faces Constitutional Problems*, Harvard Law Record, Nov. 10, 1960, pp. 9, 13.
[81] Chieftaincy Act, 1961, art. 81, § 62(2).
[82] *Id.* § 62(3).
[83] *Id.* § 63(2).
[84] *Id.* § 64.

The courts of Ghana inevitably have some leeway for creative activity in deciding cases not covered by statute. In so far as they draw inspiration for their decisions from some local custom, they may be said to have assimilated customary law into a body of national common law. This in fact is the historic method of the Anglo-American common law and its use in the new order in Ghana may reasonably be expected. On the other hand, if the generalization of customary law is left to legislation or to the procedures outlined in the Chieftaincy Act, there seems to be little reason for categorizing the resulting rule as either common law or customary law; such a rule would derive its force from the enacting statute or legislative instrument. Determination of the significance of assimilation for legal change in Ghana must await developments.

The Courts Act of 1960 repealed the old Courts Ordinance, but the common law, doctrines of equity, and statutes of general application in force in England on July 24, 1874, were retained. Section 17(1) of the new Interpretation Act defines the common law as including doctrines of equity and both were therefore retained in the new legal order of Ghana by article forty of the Republican Constitution. Statutes of general application were also retained, though somewhat circuitously. The Courts Act, section 154(4), kept in effect such statutes of general application in force in England on the cut-off date as applied in Ghana immediately before the Act became effective. Thus these statutes were preserved by the provision of article forty of the Constitution covering "enactments in force immediately before the coming into operation of the Constitution." The new Interpretation Act, section 17(3), further provides that these retained statutes of general application shall be treated as part of the common law and shall stand in the hierarchy of norms above any rule of the common law other than a rule assimilated from customary law.

The net result of this circumlocution is to preserve the statutes of general application in very nearly the same position relative to the common law which they occupied in the former hierarchy of norms, except that now they are regarded as a preferred part of the common law.

A rule of equity, in case of inconsistency, is to prevail over any rule other than an assimilated rule. Thus it might appear that in the new hierarchy of norms equity doctrines have been raised above rules derived from English statutes of general application, if the latter are treated as part of the common law. On the other hand, the statute expressly states that rules derived from statutes of general application prevail over all other parts of the common law except rules assimilated from customary law. Since equity is defined as part of the common law, this suggests that statutes of general application have retained their precedence over equity doctrine. In this regard the provisions of section 17(2) and (3) of the new Interpretation Act may appear to present inconsistent views on the hierarchy of norms. A possible reconciliation might be effected by regarding the statutes of general application as technically not part of the common law as encompassed by section 17(1), and therefore deriving priority of application only from the specific rule of section 17(3) which ranks them above all common law rules except assimilated rules.

The enactments adopted on the creation of the Republic contain a novel set of provisions dealing with the administration by the courts of a common law system. As noted earlier, part of the English legacy to the Gold Coast was the doctrine of precedent or stare decisis. In the old order there was great uncertainty as to whether the decisions of certain English courts were binding on the courts of the Gold Coast and further over the effect of their dates on the status of English decisions, that is, the significance of their having been handed down before or after the date of the reception of English law in the Gold Coast. Some clarification on these points comes from the new Constitution. The appeal previously allowed from the courts of Ghana to the Judicial Committee of the Privy Council was eliminated; the Supreme Court of Ghana thus became the tribunal of last resort.[85] Consequently after the establishment of the Republic no English court by its decision could bind the courts of Ghana. Within the hierarchy of Ghanaian courts the Constitution provides that[86]

> The Supreme Court shall in principle be bound to follow its own previous decisions on questions of law, and the High Court shall be bound to follow previous decisions of the Supreme Court on such questions, but neither Court shall be otherwise bound to follow the previous decisions of any court on questions of law.

The Interpretation Act of 1960 further provides (section 17(4)) that "in deciding upon the existence or content of a rule of the common law, as so defined, the Court may have regard to any exposition of that rule by a court exercising jurisdiction in any country."

At first impression it appears that the Supreme Court of Ghana is constitutionally committed to a doctrine of precedent similar to that in England whereby the House of Lords is bound by its own prior decisions and therefore lacks the power, normally assumed by American courts, to correct its prior mistakes by overruling previous decisions either of common law or statutory interpretation. In England, the same doctrine of judicial restraint or impotence is often said to apply to the High Court with respect to its own prior decisions. To the extent that the doctrine has been accepted in Ghana, it seems to be limited to the Supreme Court.

A question may be raised, however, as to the significance of the provision that the Supreme Court shall be bound "in principle" to its prior decisions. In prevailing common law theory, the only binding aspect of a decision for later cases is its "principle" or *ratio decidendi*. Only by determining this principle can a court fix the authority, the binding aspect of a case. In the process of articulating the principle a court, therefore, has a range of flexibility and may succeed in distinguishing the present case so that it lies outside the authoritative principle. At least this much freedom is left to the Supreme Court of Ghana. Another possible interpretation of the constitutional provision, however, would equate the phrase "in principle" to "in

---

[85] REPUBLICAN CONST. art. 42(1).   [86] *Id.* art. 42(4).

general" or "ordinarily." Such an interpretation would bring the doctrine of stare decisis in Ghana much more closely in line with that prevailing in the United States. Here the values of doctrinal stability and predictability of decisions are recognized and ordinarily are implemented. At the same time, however, these values may be sacrificed by judicial adaptation of the law to changed circumstances or by the correction of serious prior error. The pre-Republican constitutional discussions throw no light on this problem of interpretation, nor do decisions of the Supreme Court thus far.

In the pre-Republican legal order of the Gold Coast and Ghana, it was recognized that beyond the range of local and English decisions, binding under the accepted doctrine of precedent, lay a further range of English and Commonwealth decisions which might be recognized as highly persuasive. For example, in appropriate circumstances, decisions of the English High Court or House of Lords, of the East African Court of Appeal, or the Supreme Court of India might be accepted as correct declarations and applications of the law in force in Ghana as well. Despite their common legal roots, however, it is by no means common for courts in the English tradition to refer to American decisions. The possibility of greater resort to these resources is at least suggested by the Interpretation Act of 1960 which authorizes the courts of Ghana in deciding the existence or content of common law rules to "have regard to any exposition of that rule by a court exercising jurisdiction in any country." Whether this possibility will be realized can only be determined by observing the conduct of the courts of Ghana for the next several years.

Another interesting though probably academic question in the administration of Ghana's common law system concerns the power of the Supreme Court under the new dispensation to modify or abandon rules provided by the old English statutes of general application. As has been seen these are now categorized as part of the common law. Furthermore, such rules were not created by prior decisions of the Supreme Court and are not therefore protected by the stringent doctrines of precedent that one interpretation of the Constitution may have imposed on the Supreme Court. Arguably, therefore, the Supreme Court could modify them, as it might change rules forming part of the common law because laid down by prior decisions of the High Court or of English courts. This seems unlikely to occur to any considerable extent, however; such law reform will result if at all from legislation in Parliament.

The problem remains of determining the status of customary law in the new hierarchy of norms. As we have seen, the former Courts Ordinance made customary law applicable in causes between natives unless an agreement could be found to have English law apply, and in causes between natives and non-natives if the court should decide that injustice would result to either party from the strict application of English law. Understandably an effort has been made in the new legislation to abandon an avowedly ethnic criterion for determining the applicable legal rules and also to deal with the complex problems of conflict between bodies of customary law and of determining the content of customary law rules.

Standards for determining the choice between common law and customary law are provided by a series of rules in section sixty-six of the new Courts Act. The new organizing concept is that of "personal law" which is defined as the system of customary law to which a person is subject or, "if he is not shown to be subject to customary law ... the common law." The six rules must be quoted in full text:

Rule 1. Where two persons have the same personal law one of them cannot, by dealing in a manner regulated by some other law with property in which the other has a present or expectant interest, alter or affect that interest to an extent which should not in the circumstances be open to him under his personal law.

Rule 2. Subject to Rule 1, where an issue arises out of a transaction the parties to which have agreed, or may from the form or nature of the transaction be taken to have agreed, that such an issue should be determined according to the common law or any system of customary law effect should be given to the agreement.

In this rule "transaction" includes a marriage and an agreement or arrangement to marry.

Rule 3. Subject to Rule 1, where an issue arises out of any unilateral disposition and it appears from the form or nature of the disposition or otherwise that the person effecting the disposition intended that such an issue should be determined according to the common law or any system of customary law effect should be given to the intention.

Rule 4. Subject to the foregoing rules, where an issue relates to entitlement to land on the death of the owner or otherwise relates to title to land—

(a) if all the parties to the proceedings who claim to be entitled to the land or a right relating thereto trace their claims from one person who is subject to customary law, or from one family or other group of persons all subject to the same customary law, the issue should be determined according to that law;

(b) if the said parties trace their claims from different persons, or families or other groups of persons, who are all subject to the same customary law, the issue should be determined according to that law;

(c) in any other case, the issue should be determined according to the law of the place in which the land is situated.

Rule 5. Subject to Rules 1 and 3, where an issue relates to the devolution of the property (other than land) of a person on his death it should be determined according to his personal law.

Rule 6. Subject to the foregoing rules, an issue should be determined according to the common law unless the plaintiff is subject to any system of customary law and claims to have the issue determined according to that system, when it should be so determined.

The appearance of clarity and certainty presented by this catalog of rules on the choice of law problem is misleading. The use of the concept of personal law in a legal order based primarily on the concept of territoriality of laws introduces great complexity. Many of the legal norms of Ghana are applicable within the geographic boundaries of the nation. The common law and the general systems of customary law are "personal," however, and their application depends on the particular persons involved. Surprisingly the Courts Act is entirely silent as to the criteria by which one's "personal law" is to be determined. Presumably this determination must still be made on the basis of such ethnic factors as determined the jurisdiction of the former Native Courts, that is, is the person of African descent? Is his way of life that of a native community? If so, of what native community is he a member? While the legislative draftsmen were able to avoid the use of the word "native," the concept of personal law seemingly commits the courts to criteria reminiscent of the colonial period in answering the choice of law questions.

It should be observed that the new legislation actually improves the status of the common law, that is, law derived primarily from England, in its competition with indigenous legal norms. Formerly there was a presumption favoring the applicability of customary law in cases where the parties were "natives" or "of African descent." Customary law might also control in certain cases even though some of the parties were non-natives. Under the new legislation, the initial presumption favors the application of the common law in many instances where previously a contrary presumption would have prevailed. The first five rules specify bases for determining the applicability of "personal law." In these rules "personal law" seemingly is to be taken to mean the common law unless the person affected shows that he is subject to some body of customary law that provides an applicable rule.[87] This view appears to be confirmed by rule six which declares that "subject to the foregoing rules, an issue should be determined according to the common law unless the plaintiff is subject to any system of customary law and claims to have the issue determined according to that system, when it should be so determined." Thus none of the six rules on the application of "personal law" compels the court on its own initiative to seek out a basis for applying customary law. The court is entitled to apply the common law, unless the affected party establishes the propriety of applying a personal law from the indigenous systems.

A difference in the phraseology of rule six from that employed in the first five rules suggests a further limitation on the application of native custom as personal law. Rules one to five deal with the law applicable in certain property transactions and in cases where the parties have agreed, either expressly or by implication, that a certain law should apply. Within the scope of these rules, either party apparently may claim the benefit of the appropriate personal law and establish the basis for its application. In the residue of cases, covered by rule six, the literal language seemingly would entitle only the plaintiff to negative the presumption of applicability of the common law. Why the important issue of choice of law should be thus determined by the vagaries of the lineup of parties in an action is by no means clear. In any event, it appears that the earlier boundaries between the English—derived common law

[87] Section 66(1) of the Courts Act thus declares that in the several specific rules "references to the personal law of a person are references to the system of customary law to which he is subject or, if he is not shown to be subject to customary law, are references to the common law. . . ."

and customary law have been shifted and the area of the indigenous systems restricted.

One final limitation[88] of the new Courts Act on the application of customary law should be noted. Section sixty-six in conclusion provides that notwithstanding the earlier provisions of the section, which in general sought to delimit an area of application for customary law, two sets of legal rules derived from English law shall apply: (1) the rules of private international law, in any proceedings in which an issue concerning the application of law prevailing in any country outside Ghana is raised; (2) "the rules of estoppel and such other of the rules generally known as the common law and the rules generally known as the doctrines of equity as have heretofore been treated as applicable in all proceedings in Ghana shall continue to be so treated."

The first of these categories is not of primary interest here. The use of conflicts rules derived from English or other non-African law in those cases involving an issue of non-Ghanaian law would affect only a thin stratum of Ghanaian society, primarily those persons engaged in some way in international business transactions. The second category of rules is of greater general interest. The underlying premise is that in pre-Republican Ghana and the Gold Coast, certain rules derived from English common law and equity were applicable in all legal proceedings, even those otherwise governed by the indigenous customary law. All such rules are to be retained in the new legal order. What are these rules and doctrines? The statute provides only one illustration: the rules of estoppel. In general, it may be said that these rules represent particularizations by the courts of the general ideas of "natural justice, equity and good conscience" which in the old legal order set bounds to the application of customary law and also provided the basis for decision where the customary law was thought not to offer a relevant rule.

[88] A further inroad on the area of application of customary law was introduced by the Courts Act of 1960 as originally enacted. As already noted, the new Interpretation Act, § 17(1), suggested the possibility of a later enactment to provide for the assimilation by the common law of certain rules of customary law found suitable for general application. The Courts Act, § 66(2), provided that where, under any of the six rules previously discussed, customary law was applicable but a relevant rule of customary law had been assimilated by the common law, the rule thus assimilated should be applied. The effect of this provision in further curtailing the customary law may be illustrated by the following case. In Fanti law intestate succession to property is matrilineal, while the basic rule among the Ga people provides for patrilineal succession. Assume that under some legislative authorization it were determined that the Ga rule was more in keeping with the modern economic and social conditions of Ghana and should be assimilated by the common law. In a subsequent case between Fantis involving Fanti lands, the rules of § 66 of the new Courts Act would indicate that the case should be determined by Fanti customary law. However, since a "relevant" rule, that is, a rule dealing with the kind of problem presented, had been assimilated, the rule assimilated by the common law from the Ga custom would be applicable. To insist that this is still the application of "customary law" is to permit a label to blind one to substance. In so far as the Fanti parties are concerned, their custom would have been rejected in favor of a national rule. Arguably, it would in the circumstances mean no more to them that the national rule was a generalization from an African (Ga) custom than if it were derived from English law. In view of jealousies and historic differences among the indigenous people of Ghana, the nationalization of one tribal rule might be less acceptable than similar treatment of an English doctrine.

This troublesome aspect of the Courts Act has now been eliminated. Section 66(2) of the Courts Act was repealed by § 69(1) of the Chieftaincy Act, Act 81 of 1961.

In summary, it appears clear that the new legal order has not in any way enlarged the scope of application of customary law. On the contrary, in the competition between customary law and English law (common law, equity, and statutes of general application), English law seems somewhat advantaged by the new ordering. This treatment of customary law must be viewed in the larger perspective of the relations between the traditional tribal institutions and the power centers of a new national state. In the new order, the center of activity in creation and adaptation of norms will not be the judiciary administering an amorphous, pluralistic system of customary and common law, but rather the national legislature.

One further feature of the 1960 legislation must be examined. This deals with the determination of the content of customary law in cases governed by it. The earlier view regarded customary law as a matter of fact, at least in the superior courts, to be established by proof. The dictum of *Angu v. Attah*[89] had suggested that some rules might become sufficiently "notorious" through frequent proof that judicial notice might be taken of them, but this suggestion does not seem to have been followed. Section 67(1) of the Courts Act, 1960, declares, however, that the question of the existence or content of a rule of customary law is a question of law for the court and not a question of fact. The important aspect of this provision is not the clear assignment of the finding function to the court rather than to assessors or jury. Even when customary law was deemed a matter of fact, the function of finding it was assigned to the court.[90] The significant change is that customary law is to be found *as law* rather than as fact. If the normal consequences of this categorization are to prevail here, a court may determine the applicable customary law rule from its own knowledge or assumed knowledge or from investigations conducted by the court but in no way reflected in the record short of the court's announcement of the rule to be applied.

While freeing the courts from the necessity of building a record to support their findings of customary law, Parliament realistically recognized that in many instances alleged to be controlled by customary law the courts will need to inquire concerning the existence and content of the applicable norm. Under the Courts Act, section 67(2)(3), the extent and methods of inquiry are left largely to the court's discretion. Techniques suggested by the statute include considering such "submissions" as may be made by the parties, consulting reported cases, textbooks and such "other sources as may be appropriate," calling and hearing such witnesses as the court deems proper, and requesting a written opinion from a House of Chiefs, State Council, "or other body possessing knowledge of the customary law in question." It seems obvious that a court has discretion to determine which one or more of these techniques will be used.

It appears equally obvious that the court is not bound to accept any particular opinion. The statute is silent, however, as to whether a court that has decided to hear witnesses or to request written opinions on the customary law must preserve the

[89] See note 68 *supra*. [90] See Allott, *supra* note 73, at 248.

testimony and documents in the record for use by a reviewing court. No such necessity would seem to exist if customary law is indeed to be found as law and if the testimony and opinions of witnesses and the submissions of the parties are analogized to the legal memoranda or oral arguments on the law adduced in a trial court in England or the United States. Whether or not the trial court's inquiry into customary law is preserved in the record, it would appear that any reviewing court may utilize the same techniques for supplementing its assumed knowledge of customary law. A further consequence of the categorization of customary law as law would therefore be that a trial court's determination of the applicable rule would enjoy no presumption of accuracy or reliability on appeal or other review.

Experience alone will determine the actual effect of the new provisions on the finding of customary law. The initial analysis suggests the possibility that in operation they may slowly erode variable local customs in favor of a national "customary law." The similarity between the possible, clearly authorized handling of customary law in the courts of Ghana and the development of the common law in England is striking. To Blackstone the common law of England rested in general custom, but it was known and its validity determined by the judges, "the depositories of the laws; the living oracles, who must decide in all cases of doubt...."[91] Local custom, variable throughout the realm, could indeed be given effect subject to rather stringent criteria, but, when relied on, allegation and proof were in general required and the issue thus raised was ordinarily for the jury.[92] Thus the treatment of customary law under the new Courts Act of Ghana more closely resembles that of general common law in England than local custom. The commitment of the decisional function to the courts as on questions of law augurs the demise of local particularity and the emergence of a body of national Ghanaian common law.

Conclusion

To a considerable extent the actual impact of the formal changes in the structure of the operative legal norms of Ghana remains speculative. Continuing study of legislative developments and the judicial process is essential. It may be suggested, however, that the grant of independence and the adoption of a Republican form of government have not served to revitalize that part of the legal order which is derived from the indigenous societies. On the contrary, this component of the legal order seems to have suffered continued attrition in favor of legal institutions and legal norms received from non-indigenous, primarily British sources and incorporated in a rapidly growing body of national legislation.[93] In so far as "Africanization" of

---

[91] 1 William Blackstone, Commentaries on the Laws of England *69 (3d ed. 1892).
[92] Id. at *74-*76.
[93] Following the creation of the Republic a comprehensive scheme of statute law revision was begun under the general direction of the Attorney-General by a Parliamentary Draftsman on loan from the Government of Ireland with the aid of some members of the Attorney-General's staff. The purpose of the scheme was to replace all pre-July, 1960, statute law by a series of consolidating enactments in modern language. Among the statutes thus far produced are the Legal Profession Act, Arbitration Act,

the legal order is to occur, it is to be expected mainly from the activity of Parliament. The extent to which legislative reforms draw inspiration from indigenous institutions or remain more broadly eclectic can only be determined by analysis, too detailed for this paper, of enactments since independence.

Extradition Act, Judgments (International Enforcement) Act, Criminal Code, Criminal Procedure Code, Lotteries and Betting Act, Coroners Act, Notaries Public Act, Administration of Estates Act, Apprentices Act, Bills of Exchange Act, Bills of Lading Act, and Contracts Act. A major study has also been made by Professor L. C. B. Gower of the London School of Economics looking toward a comprehensive revision of the company law of Ghana. COMMISSION OF ENQUIRY INTO THE WORKING AND ADMINISTRATION OF THE PRESENT COMPANY LAW OF GHANA, ACCRA, FINAL REPORT (1961).

CUSTOMARY LAW IN THE NEW AFRICAN STATES
Lloyd Fallers[*]

INTRODUCTION

Among the long list of intractable problems faced by the new independent states of Africa, by no means the least severe is that of creating national legal systems out of the welter of indigenous and introduced bodies of law with which they come to independence. Bodies of customary law have survived, and in some cases have even been strengthened, during the period of colonial administration; European and, in some instances, Near Eastern and Asian elements have been added to the potpourri. As members of the various communities to which these diverse bodies of law apply increasingly marry, contract with, and rob one another, the potentiality for conflict of laws is enormous. In relatively few cases have satisfactory means of reconciling them been developed.

This legal pluralism is, of course, merely the legal aspect of the general cultural fragmentation which is so characteristic of the new African states. Consisting of congeries of traditional polities—some tiny clusters of a few villages, others great kingdoms numbering their subjects in the millions—thrown together by European diplomacy in the nineteenth century, the new states have little common culture to unite them. Over large areas of Asia and the Near East, and Muslim North Africa as well, otherwise diverse peoples are given a measure of unity—including sometimes unity of law—by the influence of the great multi-ethnic "world religions": Islam, Buddhism, and Hinduism. The peoples of sub-Saharan Africa, however, lack such bases for common loyalty and identification. To be sure, there is over large areas a great deal of similarity of culture and language. For example, by far the larger part of the continent south of the Sudan belt is populated by speakers of Bantu and related languages whose historical differentiation, linguists tell us, is very recent—perhaps a matter of only a very few thousand years.[1] But, not being embodied in an elite literary tradition which might have articulated and concretized them, these elements of common culture have little unifying influence to contribute to the new states. Before the establishment of colonial rule, the thousands of distinct African polities confronted one another as autonomous and often hostile entities; to a great extent, they still do.

Such unity as the sub-Saharan states possess today is in large part a product of the colonial experience—of the common Western education of the elites and of the common reaction against colonial rule and against the centuries of slavery which preceded it. This unity, however, is both a doubtful and wasting asset: doubtful

[*] Ph.B. 1946, M.A. 1949, Ph.D. 1953, University of Chicago. Associate Professor, Department of Anthropology, University of Chicago.

[1] Greenberg, *Africa as a Linguistic Area*, in William R. Bascom & Melville J. Herskovits, Continuity and Change in African Cultures (1958).

because community based upon a language and culture borrowed from the colonial rulers is ideologically unsatisfying, tending to perpetuate the sense of dependence and inferiority which so torments African leaders; and wasting because, as the years after independence roll on, feelings of brotherhood based upon common opposition tend to wane. A deeper and more enduring sense of nationhood and citizenship can only develop slowly through the confrontation of common problems and through the ideological creativity of leaders who are able to synthesize new national cultures—cultures which are modern in attitude but which also draw upon the underlying, but previously unarticulated, cultural unities of traditional Africa. Such conceptions as *"negritude"* and "African personality" may be understood as the initial and as yet rather vague attempts at such synthesis.

At present, however, the overriding cultural—and legal—reality for the vast majority of village-dwelling Africans is the traditional ethnic group. If one has in mind this tribally-oriented majority, and not the small minority whose primary loyalties are wider, then the relevant boundaries between bodies of law are not the familiar political frontiers shown on most maps but rather the many times more numerous boundaries between traditional tribes and kingdoms which appear on the maps of anthropologists.[2]

The problems of legal administration involved in reconciling these dozens—in some states, hundreds—of customary jurisdictions among themselves and with the more recently introduced bodies of law are lawyers' problems, upon which an anthropologist is very ill-equipped to comment. His specialty is rather the microscopic view—the detailed analysis of how a particular body of customary law operates today, at the moment of independence, to provide justice for ordinary members of an African community in the conflicts that commonly take them into court.[3]

On one level, such an analysis tells us only about the law of the community in question; it cannot tell us much about the substance of "African law" in general for, as the above remarks indicate, "African law" in this sense does not exist. This does not mean, however, that we can learn nothing of wider relevance from the examination of law in a particular African community. For while the substantive customary law is of local application only, the degree to which it continues to order relations among members of the community, and the ways in which it responds to changes in these relations, may be quite typical. To the extent to which this is so, an assessment of the present state of customary law in a contemporary African community may perhaps assist lawyers in thinking about the broader problems of legal pluralism at the level of the new national states. If customary law remains vigorous in the life of the people and if it is flexible enough to adapt to new circumstances, then the architects of the new national legal systems may prefer to seek means of incorporating it and equipping it with the tools for further evolution, rather than sweeping it away in a burst of legislative enthusiasm.

[2] See, for example, GEORGE P. MURDOCK, AFRICA: ITS PEOPLES AND THEIR CULTURE HISTORY (1959).
[3] Perhaps the best examples of such studies are MAX GLUCKMAN, THE JUDICIAL PROCESS AMONG THE BAROTSE (1955), and P. J. BOHANNAN, JUSTICE AND JUDGMENT AMONG THE TIV (1959).

I

A Day in Court

Perhaps the best way of conveying some sense of the present condition of customary law is by describing an actual case as it comes before a court and is adjudicated. The material that we shall present comes from Busoga District in the Eastern Province of Uganda, then a British protectorate.[4] While of course each area has its peculiarities, the position of customary law and customary courts in Busoga may be taken as broadly representative of that in most African countries presently or formerly under British administration.

The reader should imagine a long, low-thatched building—the courthouse—with whitewashed mud-and-wattle walls, open all around at window level so that those who cannot find seats on the rows of wooden benches inside can look in. Although the court is not yet in session, dozens of bicycles are stacked against the wall outside and the room is already crowded, for litigation is a pre-eminently public activity and a popular one, giving ample scope for the people's love of intricate and eloquent rhetoric. Among the majority who have come, not to participate but simply to form an appreciative audience, are gray-haired elders who through years of attendance at court have become connoisseurs of the litigious art, wide-eyed boys eager to further their legal education, and nursing mothers for whose infants such days in court will be among their earliest remembered experiences. Chickens wander, clucking, in and out of doorways; and a passing herdsman stops to listen to the proceedings, leaning against a tree while his cattle graze on the courthouse lawn.

For everyone present the experience will be not merely enjoyable but also instructive, because in the customary courts every man is his own advocate. And since one in every seven adult males is likely to appear in court as a principal each year, the lessons learned today will find ready application.[5] The audience is therefore attentive as the judges, formally attired in their long white gowns and Western-style jackets, file in and take their places at the table on the dais at the end of the hall: the sub-county chief and chairman of the court; two of the six parish[6] chiefs of the sub-county, serving on rotation; and two of a panel of elected members, also serving on rotation. As each speaker, litigant or witness, addresses the bench, he bows respectfully to the judges and speaks with as much gravity and eloquence as he can muster.

Today there come before the court two peasant farmers, Sulaiti Mukama and Kaswabuli, both of the village of Bukona.[7] They are contending for a piece of land—

---

[4] The material reported in this paper was gathered during 1950-1952, while the writer was serving as a Research Fellow of the East African Institute of Social Research. Uganda became an independent state on October 9, 1962. N.Y. Times, Oct. 9, 1962, p. 8, col. 1.

[5] This calculation is for one county of Busoga District in which the rate of litigation is not unusually high.

[6] The term "parish" has no ecclesiastical reference.

[7] Case No. 71, 1951, Sub-County Court of Ssaabawaali, County of Kigulu. The quotations given below are translations from the written case record.

a *kibanja,* as the Basoga[8] call a complete peasant's holding, with its plantain garden from which comes the staple food, its tract of fallow, and its plots for peanuts, maize, cotton, and other annual food and cash crops. Although Sulaiti Mukama is in possession of the land, he nevertheless appears as "accuser," having laid his case before the chief some days earlier and having had it entered on the docket. The reason is this: while this sub-county court is the lowest "court of record"—the lowest court recognized by the statutes of the Uganda Protectorate—there are also three lower levels of "courts" presided over, in ascending order, by the headman of the sub-village, the headman of the village, and the chief of the parish (an area containing several villages). Although no statute says it must do so, each case must, in customary practice, pass through this hierarchy of unofficial courts before reaching the sub-county court, and many are successfully arbitrated in the process. In the case before us, however, Kaswabuli has secured a favorable judgment from these lower courts and Sulaiti Mukama has refused to accept it. From the point of view of the litigants, therefore, the case comes to the sub-county court on "appeal"; and Sulaiti Mukama, who occupies the land in question, is the accuser.

As the case opens, the court clerk, who will laboriously record the proceedings in longhand in the local language, reads Sulaiti Mukama's charge against Kaswabuli: "For taking my *kibanja,* which was allotted to me by the sub-village headman, Semeyi." The court then addresses the accused, Kaswabuli:

Q: Do you agree to contest this case and do you say that you will win or lose? You do not have to answer, but anything you say will be used as evidence by the court.

Here is a charge to the accused clearly taken from British practice, but we may note that he is not sworn to truthfulness. In a peasant community it is not so much the "facts" that are in question; probably everyone knows these. Consequently, it is assumed in Busoga courts that an honorable man will lie on his own behalf; the court is expected to discover where substantial truth and justice lie through clever questioning of everyone concerned.[9]

The accused then states his case:

A: I agree to contest and I say that I will win, because Sulaiti Mukama has no *kibanja.* The *kibanja* which the headman allotted to him was mine. I inherited it from my grandfather, Kikoma, and the village headman who allotted it to him was Mwoga. After Kikoma's death my father, Nandere, took it, and after my father's death, I inherited it. But since my father died while I was still young, the sub-village headman, Semeyi, tried to take part of it to give to Sulaiti Mukama. When I grew up, I accused the sub-village headman before the village headman and I won the case. The village

---

[8] The country is called "Busoga," the people "Basoga."
[9] There are exceptions to this: When a man addresses the court as a formal witness to a contract, he is expected to tell the truth.

headman sent representatives, who marked out and returned to me the part which had been given to Sulaiti Mukama. Eria Bakali is my witness who can prove that the *kibanja* is mine.

Having heard from Kaswabuli, the court returns to Sulaiti Mukama, the accuser, and similarly charges him: "Do you agree to contest . . . ."

A: I agree to contest and I say that I shall win, because the *kibanja* is mine. It was given to me by the sub-village headman, Semeyi, and I have spent twenty-eight years in it. When he says that he went and accused me to the village headman, he is lying. He only went to inform the village headman in a friendly way and the village headman made a case of it. From the information he had from Kaswabuli, the headman sent some representatives to go and give Kaswabuli the *kibanja*. But the sub-village headman who had given it to me, Semeyi, was not present when they uprooted the old boundary trees and planted new ones. All these things were done also in my absence, while I was on a journey. But when I returned I made a case against them in the parish chief's court and he called the village headman and Kaswabuli, but they refused to appear. To further prove that the *kibanja* presently in question is mine, Kaswabuli successfully claimed the neighboring *kibanja* at the time of Semeyi's death and was given representatives from this court to plant boundary trees for him. Another thing that proves it is that Kaswabuli has never taken the matter of this piece of land before the lineage council of Semeyi, the sub-village headman who allotted the land to me, since Semeyi's death. Walajja is my witness who can prove that the *kibanja* is mine, for he is the one who allotted it to me.

Now both principals have stated their cases and the court must proceed to question them and their witnesses in order to arrive at a decision. Meanwhile, however, there are elements in the initial statements which we cannot understand without further information. In order to appreciate what these statements will have meant to the court and the lines of questioning which it will now follow, we must explain some of the elements of land law and village government in Busoga.

It will have been clear from the initial statements that a number of parties are involved in the distribution of rights in land. Both principals have spoken of the land having been "allotted" by sub-village headmen. Kaswabuli has spoken of "inheriting" the land. Sulaiti Mukama has charged Kaswabuli with not "taking the matter to the lineage council" and has confused us by referring to two different men as the headman by whom he was allotted the land. Also, both village and sub-village headmen seem to have been involved. What does all this mean?

First of all, each village in Busoga has a hereditary headman, and each is divided into sub-villages, also with hereditary headmen. A peasant who wishes to take up land goes to the sub-village headman who, if he has a vacant plot in his area, may allot it to him in exchange for a sum of money and a symbolic payment of a chicken in recognition of the headman's overlordship. When the peasant dies, the land passes to his heir without further reference to the sub-village headman, but if he should die without leaving an heir or leave the land vacant for more than a season or two, the headman may repossess the land for allotment to someone else. The headman of the whole village should be notified of, and give his consent to, allotments made by his sub-village headmen. "Inheritance," in the case of both the peasant's plot and the headman's office, means inheritance within a patrilineal descent group—a lineage; but there is no fixed order of succession. The emphasis is upon the corporate rights of the lineage, not the right of the individual to succession. The lineage council, which meets at the funeral feast a few weeks after a man's death, may choose any of his sons, or even brothers or brothers' sons, whom it may regard as most suitable to be heir. Since rights in land and office thus reside ultimately in the lineage as a corporation, a person who has a claim against the deceased should present it before the council meeting at the funeral feast. Sulaiti Mukama is arguing that if Kaswabuli had a valid claim against land allocated by Semeyi, the sub-village headman, he should have pressed it at Semeyi's death. This same emphasis upon the rights of the lineage appears in Sulaiti Mukama's reference to both Semeyi and Walajja as the "headman who allotted the land to me." Semeyi has died and Walajja is his successor; the identification is so complete that Walajja may be spoken of as having done things, in his official capacity, that were actually done by his predecessor.

Thus, rights in a piece of land are distributed among six parties: the village headman, the sub-village headman, the peasant cultivator, and the respective lineages of all three. Several of these rights have been asserted in the initial statements of the litigants and the court must now determine who, on balance, is entitled to possession. In its pursuit of a decision (an *ensala,* a "cutting," Basoga call it, conceptualizing the court's task as one of "cutting through" a tangle of argument and counter-argument), the judges now question the witnesses brought by the litigants.

Walajja, Sulaiti Mukama's witness, says nothing new, merely confirming that Semeyi allotted the land to Sulaiti Mukama and that the latter has occupied it undisturbed for twenty-eight years. Kaswabuli's witness, Eria Bakali, also confirms the testimony of his principal, saying that Kaswabuli inherited the land from his father and grandfather. He adds, however, a statement which may be significant: "When Nandere (Kaswabuli's father) died, he left the land in the hands of his wife, Mpoyendeza, to keep for his son. When Semeyi, the headman, saw that it was in the hands of a mere woman, he cut part of it and gave it to Sulaiti Mukama...."

Here is a possible lead: the victimization of a poor widow and her child. In the customary law, a minor heir is secure in his rights so long as an adult is named by the lineage as his guardian and trustee. If Semeyi, the headman, took the land from a legitimate minor heir, then the beneficiary of his action has no valid right to the land. The court is aware that this kind of skulduggery on the part of headmen is not uncommon; since the headmen get no further income from the land under their jurisdiction so long as it passes down a line of heirs, they sometimes illegitimately seize the land of a minor heir in order to allot it to a new tenant, from whom an allotment fee will be forthcoming. Turning to Walajja, Sulaiti Mukama's witness, the court asks:

> Q: From whom did Semeyi get the land which he gave to Sulaiti Mukama?
> A: From the old woman, Mpoyendeza.

Here seems to be confirmation, but, curiously, this is not the line which the court pursues. Leaving Sulaiti Mukama, whose position would have been damaged by evidence of such a course of events, it turns to Kaswabuli, who claims to have inherited as a minor:

> Q: Before Semeyi died, did you ever accuse him for allotting your *kibanja* to someone else?
> A: I didn't because I was still young.
> Q: Sulaiti Mukama says that when Semeyi died you dealt with the matter of another *kibanja* and that you were given it. Is that so?
> A: Yes, we dealt with it and I won.
> Q: Why did you not at the time deal with both plots of land if you knew both were yours?
> A: Because the first *kibanja* for which I claimed was taken from me by the village headman, not the sub-village headman Semeyi.
> Q: You at first said that Sulaiti had no *kibanja* and now you say that one was given to him by the sub-village headman, Semeyi. Has he two for which you are claiming, the one you are taking and the one given to him by Semeyi?
> A: He has only one, the one given him by Semeyi.
> Q: Is that the one in which he says he has spent twenty-eight years?
> A: That is the one.
> Q: We have heard you say that you were still young at that time, but when did you become old enough to understand the affair of the *kibanja*?
> A: I learned all about it in 1935 (sixteen years earlier).

Pressing this line of inquiry, the court turns to Walajja, the sub-village headman and Sulaiti Mukama's witness:

> Q: How old was Kaswabuli at his father's death?
> A: He had already paid poll tax.[10]

And then to Eria Bakali, Kaswabuli's witness:

> Q: In what year did Semeyi give land to Sulaiti Mukama?
> A. I don't remember the year.

[10] He was therefore at least eighteen years of age.

By now, both the witness and his principal will have realized what is coming and the witness evades a question to which he almost certainly knows the answer very well. But the court presses the attack:

> Q: After the death of Semeyi, did Kaswabuli take the matter before the council of Semeyi's lineage?
> A: Yes, he took it before Ziyadi, the lineage head, and Ziyadi demanded a chicken to settle it.[11]
> Q: Kaswabuli says that he did not take the matter of the *kibanja* before the lineage council and now you say he did. Whom shall we regard as telling the truth?

Caught in an inconsistency born of panic, the witness admits that his principal "is telling the truth."

Now the court is satisfied, and after a brief discussion the unanimous decision is given:

> The case has been decided and it has gone against the accused, Kaswabuli. In his statement, he has not agreed that it goes against him. The sub-village headman, Walajja, who gave the land to the accuser, and also the witness of the accused, Eria Bakali, have agreed that since Sulaiti Mukama was given the *kibanja* twenty-eight years have passed.[12] That is why the case has been decided against the accused. The accuser is given his land. The accused has thirty days in which to appeal to the county court.[13]

Although there is good evidence that Sulaiti Mukama acquired the land through an illegitimate transaction and that Kaswabuli was at that time its rightful owner, the latter's right, the court holds, has lapsed with the passage of time. Kaswabuli has "slept on his remedy."

II

The Present and Future Position of the Customary Law

An examination of this case provides us with a brief glimpse into the actual day-to-day operation of the customary law in a contemporary African community—a background against which we may consider more broadly its present and future position.

First of all, it will have become apparent that what is going on in this court room is not simply the application of indigenous law by an indigenous court, unmodified by external forces. The proceedings exhibit many marks of British influence, the result of sixty years of colonial administration. If we are to think realistically about such courts and such law, we must understand the nature of this influence.

---

[11] The chicken is a customary symbolic payment to a judge in recognition of his authority.
[12] Eria Bakali did not actually agree, but the court knows that he is aware of the fact.
[13] Kaswabuli did not appeal.

As in most African territories administered by Great Britain, indigenous courts in Uganda have been recognized, and their functions circumscribed, by a series of ordinances, the latest in the case of Uganda being the African Courts Ordinance of 1956. Traditional Busoga was divided among a number of small, but culturally very similar kingdoms, ranging in population from a few thousand to well over one hundred thousand persons.[14] Each kingdom was headed by an hereditary ruler and each was divided into areas administered by chiefs who were the ruler's clients. Both rulers and chiefs exercised judicial as well as general administrative authority over the people under their jurisdiction, and the two kinds of authority were closely related. The gathering of subordinates in a chief's or ruler's audience hall was a *"lukiiko"*—a gathering to *"kukiika,"* to "pay homage," and to transact whatever judicial or administrative business was at hand. With the coming of British administration, the District was unified under an African Local Government; and the rulers and chiefs—who were also judges—became its civil servants. Successive courts ordinances, and the rules promulgated under them, recognized courts at what were essentially the traditional levels—now defined as "counties" and "sub-counties"—with the chief at each level as chairman; and also established a district court for Busoga as a whole. Although the traditional courts at the lower levels—the village and sub-village headmen's courts—were not formally recognized, they continued to function, as we have seen. Each court of record was given appellate jurisdiction over the courts below it as well as original jurisdiction in successively more serious cases. The whole hierarchy was placed under the revisionary and appellate jurisdiction of the British magistrate's court and the High Court of Uganda. In recent years, a beginning has been made toward separating the judiciary from the administration by appointing special judges, though these have thus far been men drawn from the ranks of the chiefs.

Subject to certain limitations, however, these reorganized courts have been directed by the ordinances to apply "native law and custom," both substantive and procedural, and the British magistrates and High Court judges have been extremely cautious in the exercise of their revisionary and appellate powers in matters of customary law. The customary courts may not try capital cases and may not apply any law which is contrary "to natural justice and morality" or to Protectorate statutes, but the British administration has been content to draw these broad limits and has not attempted to codify or substantively alter the customary law in the spheres which have been left to it. This has meant that in such important fields as land law and family law, the customary courts have throughout the sixty years of British rule exercised an essentially unrestricted jurisdiction.

Legislative enactment and appellate jurisdiction are not, of course, the only sources of British influence. British administrative officers have supervised the courts to the extent of examining their case records—thereby assuring the rather surprisingly high level of recording illustrated in the case discussed above—and have undoubtedly

[14] See generally LLOYD A. FALLERS, BANTU BUREAUCRACY (1956).

influenced substantive law to some degree through their contacts with chiefs while touring the District. Equally important perhaps, but also difficult to assess, are the consequences of the chiefs' participation in the proceedings of the British magistrates' courts and the High Court. It is the practice in these courts, when Africans appear as litigants, to invite chiefs to sit as "assessors" to advise the court on matters of custom. In the process, as the writer discovered in his conversations with chiefs, the latter observe British court practice and are influenced by it in their conduct of cases in their own courts. Some of the phrases in the case record discussed above which sound like translations of British formulae may be traceable to such experiences.

What we see in operation today, therefore, is a system of courts and a body of law which have deep roots in traditional society and culture but which have been modified, particularly in the direction of more regular organization and procedure, by years of colonial administration. It is significant that such modifications have been slight enough and gradual enough so that the Basoga may feel that these are still their courts and their law. Certainly to the outside observer this appears to be true. One may sit, day after day, observing the courts in action, with very little sense of the intrusion of foreign elements, for these elements—to the considerable extent to which they exist—have been quite thoroughly absorbed. Perhaps the clearest illustration of the care taken by the British administration to protect the integrity of the customary law is provided by the position of customary marriage. A large majority of the Basoga are Christians who contract marriages under the Marriage Ordinance, but the same large majority continue simultaneously to contract customary marriages as well, through the payment of bridewealth. The Protectorate authorities have insisted upon keeping the two processes legally distinct, maintaining the application of customary law to the bridewealth contract irrespective of proceedings regarding the same marriage which may be undertaken under the Ordinance, and have in practice ignored in the case of Africans the prohibition against polygyny which, strictly speaking, should apply to all persons married under the ordinance.

Thus the customary law remains a vigorous and efficient instrument for the adjudication of disputes, particularly in spheres such as land-holding and marriage which are most closely bound up with the village social order. But of course this social order is changing. Important as it is to maintain the continuity and integrity of the law, it is equally important, especially in a society which aspires to rapid modernization, for the law to be sufficiently flexible to adapt to new circumstances.

The courts in Busoga have demonstrated a good deal of such flexibility. For example, prior to Western contact and the spread of literacy, there was in the law of Busoga a quite highly-developed set of rules for establishing the validity of contracts through the oral testimony of witnesses.[15] As literacy has spread, the courts have apparently quite spontaneously developed new criteria for dealing with

[15] These rules are still applied to illiterates.

written documents, such as contracts and simple maps, which have now become a standard feature of marriage and land transactions. Another example is provided by the problems of time limitation—the issue upon which decision in the case discussed above turned. Today all Basoga are no longer peasant farmers. Many spend part of their lives in urban employment, and during World War II many served in the armed forces. As a result of these changes in the occupational structure, there are now new reasons why a man may delay in seeking his rights in inherited land; and particularly since the war, the courts have been developing new criteria in this area.

Thus there is little evidence of a rooted conservatism resistant to the forces of change. But adaptation requires more than a willingness to change; it also requires techniques for maintaining a satisfactory degree of consistency and unity in the law as the various courts applying it encounter and respond to new problems. In the Anglo-American legal tradition, such consistency is maintained through systems of reporting by means of which courts are made aware of precedent-setting decisions. The sixty-odd courts of Busoga form an appellate hierarchy and the notion of precedent is appreciated, but there is no systematic reporting of the decisions of the district court to the lower courts.[16] As a result, courts in various parts of the District, beginning from a common basis of customary law, may develop divergent adaptations to new conditions. There is evidence that this has happened in the sphere of land law in areas around towns where land is being put to new uses and where forms of buying and selling unknown to traditional customary law are growing up *ad hoc*. At present a number of countries are experimenting with reporting systems to meet such difficulties.[17]

However, the problems involved in developing effective systems of reporting are formidable. For the case records, admirable as they are in terms of completeness, do not readily lend themselves to analysis and abstraction. African customary law is an excellent example of what Max Weber called "substantive legal rationality."[18] Decisions are reached by judges on the basis of an implicit body of normative rules which may be highly consistent internally, but these rules are very seldom made explicit and formally manipulated in the decisions that are rendered. The case discussed above is a splendid illustration of this. The decision states only the barest essentials of the court's reasoning, merely noting that, since Kaswabuli had waited twenty-eight years to claim his rights, the case had gone against him. No mention is made of Kaswabuli's argument, to which the court had devoted a good deal of attention in its quesioning, nor of the process by which the court had concluded that Kaswabuli had neglected to sufficiently press his case.

---

[16] The writer's information on this point may be out of date, but it is safe to say that no *effective* reporting system exists.
[17] Tanganyika and Kenya, for example.
[18] Max Rheinstein (Ed.), Max Weber on Law in Economy and Society at xlviii (1954). Weber's category of "irrational" (or perhaps "non-rational") might seem more appropriate in view of the implicitness of the reasoning involved, but these terms seem to do violence to the highly consistent system of norms which underlies this implicit reasoning.

In order to determine the complete line of reasoning of a customary court and the full implications of its decision, one must carefully examine and interpret the whole body of testimony. So long as the courts operate with a static or only very slowly changing body of law and set of environing social conditions, this does not matter. But the clear statement and communication of a precedent-setting decision in response to a new problem requires, if such decisions are not to be random departures from tradition, much more explicit formulation of what is being done. The present judges in customary courts are generally incapable of this. While he was studying the customary law of Busoga, the writer found judges unwilling or unable to discuss abstract rules of law, generally responding to his questions by saying that a rule could not be stated in the absence of all the facts of the case. The study, therefore, had to be conducted almost exclusively by inference from decided cases. This kind of inferential analysis would seem to be impossibly laborious and slow for anyone charged with systematic case reporting.

Thus an important requirement for the future health of the customary law would appear to be the development of a corps of judges and clerks well trained in the existing practice of the courts, but trained also in somewhat more analytical modes of legal reasoning. There are, of course, dangers here; care must be taken to avoid arid legalism and the indiscriminate importation of alien concepts not fully understood. But granting these dangers, a somewhat more professionalized bench would nevertheless seem essential if customary law is to be made explicit enough so that its underlying principles may be applied systematically to the new circumstances that will increasingly face it. No doubt there will also arise problems to which the customary law cannot even in the best of circumstances be successfully adapted, and to which, consequently, legislation will be the only answer. But its native tradition of litigation, rooted in the structure of village life, is one of Africa's greatest cultural achievements; and it would seem a pity not to make use of it wherever possible.

Conclusion

It is well to remind ourselves, in conclusion, that bodies of customary law of the kind that we have been considering do not stand alone and self-contained in the new states. As we noted at the outset, these states each contain many bodies of such law, and Uganda is no exception to this pattern. At least a dozen distinct customary legal systems exist there, along with elements of British, Indian, and Islamic law—all under the ultimate jurisdiction of the superordinate magistrates' courts and the High Court. Perhaps the most difficult problem of all will be to devise ways of resolving the conflicts of laws that inevitably arise in such situations, while at the same time allowing the customary systems to operate in those homogeneous rural communities to which they are most suitable and which will remain for years to come the social milieu of the majority of Africans.[19]

[19] See Cowen, *African Legal Studies—A Survey of the Field and the Role of the United States*, *supra* p. 545, at 552-59; Anderson, *The Future of Islamic Law in British Commonwealth Territories in Africa*, *infra*, p. 617.

THE FUTURE OF ISLAMIC LAW IN BRITISH COMMONWEALTH TERRITORIES IN AFRICA

J. N. D. ANDERSON*

INTRODUCTION

Two questions are not infrequently asked by those who approach the subject of the continued application of Islamic law in the emergent countries of Africa with a general idea of the nature of that law but a limited acquaintance with legal developments, during the last century or more, in the Middle East, the Indian subcontinent, and the dependent or formerly dependent territories of East and West Africa. The first concerns the practicability of maintaining a situation under which different members of the same national state are subject to different systems of law. Can a modern society, it is asked, long remain viable if its legal system enshrines an interpersonal conflict of laws? The second involves the very nature of Islamic law and the possibility of its adaptation to modern life. Can an authoritative law, which is regarded as firmly based on divine revelation, so adapt itself—or be adapted—as to enable it to resolve the typical conflicts of an industrial society?

I

THE NATURE OF ISLAMIC LAW

According to the classical theory of Islamic jurisprudence, the Sharī'a, or divine law, was derived from four main sources: from the Qur'ān, as the *ipsissima verba* of Almighty God; from the Sunna or practice of the Prophet, as equally inspired in content if not in form, and as established by a multitude of traditions as to what he said, did, and allowed to be done; from the Ijmā or consensus of the doctors of the law, as yet another guarantee of the divine will; and from Qiyās, or the analogical deductions of the jurists from these primary sources. It is true that recent research has demonstrated that Islamic law as we know it was not, for the most part, deduced directly from the sacred sources but rather evolved by a succession of jurists who worked through the customary law and administrative practice of the first century of the Hijra, adopting, adapting, and discarding such law and practice on the basis of Islamic norms.[1] But this is less significant for our immediate purpose than the fact that the overwhelmingly greater part of the law was based even in the classical theory on the analogical deductions of the jurists, as authenticated, in some cases, by an alleged consensus. For the Qur'ān includes comparatively few verses of directly

* B.A. 1930, LL.B. 1931, M.A. 1934, LL.D. 1955, M.B.E. 1943, O.B.E. 1945. Professor of Oriental Laws and Director of the Institute of Advanced Legal Studies, University of London. Author, ISLAMIC LAW IN AFRICA (1954); ISLAMIC LAW IN THE MODERN WORLD (1959); and contributor of numerous articles on this subject.

[1] Compare, in particular, JOSEPH SCHACHT, THE ORIGINS OF MUHAMMADAN JURISPRUDENCE (1950).

legal significance, while the vast majority of traditions attributed to the Prophet are of distinctly dubious authenticity even by Muslim standards—quite apart from the devastating criticism to which they have been subjected by Western scholars.[2]

Until the end of the third century of the Hijra, indeed, any adequately qualified jurist was regarded as entitled to go back to the original sources of the law and to make his own deductions. It was only with the crystallization of the different "schools" of law and the consequent elaboration of the doctrine of consensus that the "door of independent deduction" came to be regarded as, in practice, closed.[3] Even so, the Islamic law was very far from being one and indivisible. Instead, there were a variety of "orthodox" schools, of which only four ultimately survived; there were a number of "heterodox" schools formed by those who are commonly regarded as sectaries; and there was a multitude of variant opinions held by different jurists within the recognized schools, professed by leaders of extinct schools, or attributed to authorities who preceded their formation.

Not only so, but in the early decades of the Muslim conquests the subjugated peoples were largely left to their own laws and their own legal institutions, while the needs of their Arab conquerors were met by the appointment of an official who can be regarded as a sort of legal secretary to the governor of the province. In course of time, however, the office of Qāḍī or judge came to be filled by those pious experts through whose efforts the Islamic law came into being; and their judicial discretion became more and more rigidly bound by its requirements. But while the resultant law was all inclusive in its scope, and while in theory it was all equally authoritative, it is undeniable that some parts were more jealously regarded and more meticulously applied than were others.

This is attributable in part to the fact that this law was evolved as an annunciation of theoretical propositions and hypothetical distinctions largely divorced from everyday practice (for the rigid prohibition of fixed rates of interest or of speculative contracts was far removed from the actual life of the markets); in part to the circumstance that no Muslim ruler seems to have been content to leave the maintenance of public order and the administration of criminal justice exclusively to those courts which were tied, both in matters of procedure and substantive law, to its meticulous requirements; and in part to the fact that the constitutional law was largely an *ex post facto* rationalization of historical developments. As a consequence, other jurisdictions in fact grew up from an early date alongside that of the Qāḍīs, and it was chiefly in the sphere of family relations and the law of succession—together with civil wrongs, basic contracts, and parts of the criminal law—that the Sharīʻa was meticulously applied. For it has always been the law of marriage and succession

[2] Here, again, Professor Schacht must be regarded as the leading authority. *Cf.* SCHACHT, *op. cit. supra* note 1.

[3] In theory, it is true, the possibility of a jurist appearing who was qualified to exercise the right of independent deduction was not excluded, but the necessary qualifications were put almost impossibly high.

which has been regarded by Muslims as most intimately connected with the practice of their religion.

Yet, at the same time, the Sharī'a was universally acclaimed as the only law, to which ruler and people were alike—and uniquely—subject; and those customary practices and administrative regulations which were enforced by officials, police, or merchants were never accorded any comparable status. As for the Sharī'a itself, this was largely moribund; for in each of the schools a dominant doctrine on most points had slowly asserted itself and was regarded as binding on future generations. The law was not entirely static, because new situations would inevitably arise; but for the most part legal scholarship found its expression in the compilation of endless commentaries and glosses on previous commentaries and glosses.

II

LAW REFORM IN ISLAMIC COUNTRIES

Such was the position throughout the vast majority of the Muslim world until little more than a century ago. But since then major developments have taken place almost everywhere. In the Ottoman Empire these started with the Tanzīmāt reforms, and took the form of the promulgation of frankly secular codes of Western origin—such as the Commercial Code in 1850 and the Penal Code in 1858—and the establishment of a secular (Niẓāmīya) system of courts to apply them. Henceforth the Sharī'a courts were to be confined to the law of family relations and succession in their widest connotation. But it is noteworthy that whereas the resultant dichotomy between the courts was complete, the dichotomy in the law they applied was mitigated by the fact that the Ottoman Law of Obligations (the Majalla) represented a codification of precepts drawn not from Western law but from the Sharī'a. In Egypt, too, which had attained juridical independence under the Khedive Ismā'īl, a similar dichotomy was effected in the courts and—less completely—in the law they were to apply. For it is noteworthy that, at this stage, it was generally considered preferable to leave the Sharī'a intact and immutable, even if this meant displacing it in one particular after another by a law of wholly alien inspiration, rather than to allow any profane meddling with its sacred precepts.

In "British" India, events took a course which was in some respects similar and in others different. As in the Ottoman Empire and Egypt, the Sharī'a law—as applied under the Moghul Emperors and the East India Company—was progressively displaced by a series of enactments such as the Indian Penal Code, Evidence Act, Contract Act, and the Transfer of Property Act. The Sharī'a law became largely limited to matters of family relations and succession in respect of Muslim litigants. Unlike the Ottoman Empire and Egypt, however, there was no corresponding dichotomy in the courts. Instead, the same courts administered whatever law was applicable in any particular case.

More recently, there have been further developments. Right up till 1915 the

Sharī'a law was administered throughout the Ottoman Empire in the traditional way, with the dominant view in the Ḥanafī school in unique ascendance; but in that year the pressure of social conditions made reforms in the Sharī'a law itself inevitable. The dike thus breached, a series of most interesting reforms have been introduced—first in Turkey and then in one after another of the Arab countries—by which the law of family relations and succession has been brought much more closely into line with the requirements of modern life. But it is important to observe that this has been done, not by the earlier expedient of displacing the Sharī'a in favor of a codified law of Western inspiration, but rather by a number of ingenious expedients by which reforms have been effected in the sacred law itself as administered by the courts without—in theory, at least—affecting its Islamic character and authority. Some of these expedients will demand more detailed notice later; but for the present it is enough to remark that they have resulted in a partial—or sometimes comparatively complete—codification of the relevant precepts. And it should be observed that much the same phenomenon appeared in British India in the Dissolution of Muslim Marriages Act, 1939, and—more recently—in the Pakistan Muslim Family Laws Ordinance, 1961.[4]

Inevitably, however, these significant developments in the law of personal status have led to a new attitude towards the rest of the law. Gone is the day when it was considered sacrilegious to tamper in any way with the sacred law, even if this meant putting it on one side in practice in favor of laws of Western inspiration. Instead there has been an increasing demand in Middle East countries to make a wider use of their own cultural heritage, together with an insistence—on the part of a somewhat vocal minority—that an adequate code for all the requirements of modern life could be derived from the Sharī'a alone, provided only that its riches were exploited in a sufficiently radical manner. New Civil Codes have, in fact, been promulgated in a number of Arab countries; but while considerable publicity has been given to their debt to the Islamic sources, it is noteworthy that in practice the Egyptian Civil Code of 1948 (which has been largely adopted in Syria and Libya) remains substantially French in its origin, while the Iraq Civil Code of 1953 represents a fusion between the Egyptian Civil Code and the Majalla.

Yet a further consequence of the progressive codification of the specifically "Islamic" law which is still applied in most Middle Eastern countries—in so far as Muslim litigants are concerned—in all matters of family relations and succession, is an increasing tendency towards the unification of the courts. The sharp dichotomy which emerged about a century ago between the old Sharī'a courts and the new secular courts was powerfully reinforced and perpetuated by the essentially different training required by those who presided and practiced in each. Almost from the first, the secular courts were staffed by personnel educated in a modern law school of the Western type, while the judges and advocates of the Sharī'a courts, who still

---

[4] Gazette of Pakistan Extraordinary, March 2, 1961.

needed to extract the dominant Ḥanafī (or Mālikī) opinion from a plethora of medieval texts, could only be drawn from those trained in the traditional manner. But as soon as the family law, too, came to be codified, the situation completely changed; for it now became almost as easy for the graduates of a modern law school to administer the law of family relationships as to apply the Commercial Code or the Penal Code.

As a consequence, the courts have been unified in recent years in both Egypt and Tunisia;[5] and although the fact that the existing personnel of the Sharī'a courts have for the most part been absorbed in the national courts has meant that little change has up till now been effected, it seems clear that in the future no more judges or advocates will be recruited from those trained in the traditional way. And it appears likely that the increasing pressures of nationalism and bureaucracy will lead other Arab countries to contemplate a similar unification of their courts.

Yet the fact remains that, in almost all these countries, a different law of family relations is still applied according to the religion of the litigants. In parts of the Arabian peninsula, it is true, no law other than the law of Islam is given any official recognition; in Turkey, the Sharī'a was abandoned in 1926 in favor of the Swiss law of marriage and succession; and in Tunisia the Jewish community has voluntarily accepted the Law of Personal Status, 1956. But in most of the Arab countries no attempt has been made[6] to unify the law of marriage and divorce, or even, in some countries, the law of testate and intestate succession. So the law properly applicable to the litigants, whether codified or not, is still applied either by the appropriate community courts or by the unified national courts which have taken their place in Egypt. And this is also true, of course, in India and Pakistan, where the personal or religious law of the litigants is still applied in all such matters.

III

ISLAMIC LAW IN BRITISH AFRICA

A. The Typical Hierarchy of Legal Norms

When we turn to those countries in East and West Africa which have known British rule, we find a situation which—for all its differences—is not wildly dissimilar. It is true that some of these countries were conquered or ceded, while others may be regarded as having been settled. But in every case it has been recognized that the British settlers and officials have brought their own law with them, in so far as local circumstances may permit, while the indigenous populations have retained their existing law—except where this was regarded as contrary to natural justice, has been specifically replaced by legislation, or has been displaced in practice by the more sophisticated immigrant system. Thus the relevant Order in Council commonly provides for a Court of Record with "full jurisdiction, civil and criminal, over all

[5] The same intention has still more recently been announced in Iraq.
[6] It is true, however, that this has at times been discussed.

persons and all matters," to be exercised in accordance with the "common law, the doctrines of equity and statutes of general application in force in England" on a specified date.[7] At the same time, however, it is explicitly laid down that this imported law "shall be in force . . . so far only as the circumstances of the Territory and its inhabitants . . . permit, and subject to such qualifications as local circumstances may render necessary";[8] and it is also provided that,[9]

In all cases, civil and criminal, to which natives are parties, every Court shall (a) be guided by native law so far as it is applicable and is not repugnant to justice and morality or inconsistent with any Order in Council or Ordinance . . . ; and (b) decide all such cases according to substantial justice without undue regard to technicalities of procedure and without undue delay.

The reference to ordinance law points, of course, to the major source of legal development in each of these countries, whether dependent or independent. For the overwhelming majority of changes in the law has been introduced everywhere by local legislation, whether this was promulgated by the Governor, by the Governor in Council, by the democratic procedures of a Legislative Council or House of Assembly, or by the procedures suitable to an independent country.

But all this primarily concerns the system of courts of directly British inspiration—*i.e.*, the magistrates' courts, the Supreme or High Court, and the different courts of appeal. The overwhelmingly greater part of all litigation which concerns Africans, however, is conducted in a system of courts which are termed "native," "local," "African" or "customary," according to the territory concerned. Provision for these has in each case been made by local ordinances, under which a whole hierarchy of such courts has been set up. Sometimes, as in Kenya, there is no link whatever between the "British" and the "African" systems of courts; sometimes, as in Tanganyika, an exceedingly tenuous link has been forged; and sometimes, as in Nigeria, the two systems have been fully integrated.

Broadly speaking, moreover, the law administered by the "native" courts is precisely the "native law and custom" to which reference has already been made. As a consequence, their jurisdiction is commonly limited to "natives"—a term which is somewhat differently defined from territory to territory—while provision is sometimes made for including such immigrants as have adopted the manner of life of the indigenous inhabitants, or for excluding—in some respects—such natives as may have abandoned that manner of life. In addition, the native courts regularly enforce local legislation, in the form of Native Authority Orders, and even territorial legislation, in the form of such Ordinances, or parts of Ordinances, as they have been specifically empowered to apply.

[7] However, it should be observed that in several of the East African colonies and protectorates provision is made for jurisdiction to be exercised in conformity with the Civil and Criminal Procedure Codes of India, and other Indian Acts, and only thereafter in accordance with the Common Law.
[8] See, *e.g.*, Tanganyika Order in Council, 1920, § 17.
[9] *Id.* § 24.

B. The Place of Islamic Law

But where, it may pertinently be asked, does the Islamic law fit into this picture? And how, and to what degree, does it come to be applied in East and West Africa? The best illustration, perhaps, is provided by the way in which Roman-Dutch law originally developed. Here the process seems to have been somewhat as follows: In those parts of Northern Europe where this system came into being, a customary law of Germanic origin previously prevailed. Then, from a certain date, the rediscovered Roman law began to infiltrate, chiefly through the influence of the Church and the universities. Still later, the Roman law was officially "received." But it never, in reality, succeeded in completely displacing the existing customary law: instead, it became fused with the existing law, and a sort of amalgam of the two systems evolved.

Almost exactly the same sort of process has taken place in regard to customary law and the Islamic law in the different parts of Africa. Islam has penetrated, or is still penetrating, many parts of the continent, and the influence of Islamic law has been widely spread, superficially at least, through Muslim merchants and members of the religious orders. As a result the indigenous customary law has been leavened, in certain areas, by Islamic principles and precepts—to a degree which differs widely, of course, from place to place. In certain areas, moreover, it has been virtually displaced by the law of Islam, particularly where a native ruler has attempted to impose this law upon his people. But nowhere in tropical Africa has the imposition been complete, for traces of the customary law survive even in the most rigidly Muslim areas.

1. *Ghana, Sierra Leone, Uganda, and Nyasaland*

British territories in Africa may, in fact, be divided into those in which the Islamic law and the customary law are treated as largely identical—or at least as an indistinguishable amalgam—and those in which Islamic law is regarded as a third, distinct system, alongside the English and the indigenous law. Examples of the former may be found in Ghana, Sierra Leone, Uganda, and Nyasaland—except, that is, within the scope of certain ordinances which provide for the Islamic law to be applied, as such, in these territories in certain prescribed matters: *e.g.*, the Marriage of Mohammedans Ordinance, 1905, in Sierra Leone (but this applies only to the Colony of Freetown, not the Protectorate); the Marriage and Divorce of Mohammedans Ordinance, 1906, in Uganda (but this excludes any provisions regarding succession); and the Asiatics Marriage and Divorce Ordinance, 1929, in Nyasaland (but this, by definition, does not apply to indigenous Muslims). More surprisingly, Northern Nigeria—where the Islamic law was, until very recently, more extensively applied than anywhere else in Africa—fell within this category until the Native Courts Law and Moslem Court of Appeal Law, both of 1956, introduced for the first time an explicit distinction between the Islamic law and the customary law.

2. Somaliland, Kenya, and Zanzibar

Examples of territories where the Islamic law is regarded as a third, distinct system, on the other hand, are provided by the former British Somaliland, Kenya, and Zanzibar. In Somaliland both Qāḍīs' courts and other subordinate courts co-exist, the one applying the Islamic and the other the customary law, each within fairly well-defined limits. In Kenya, again, Muslim courts are found, chiefly in the coastal Protectorate, alongside African tribunals, while there is also a Marriage and Divorce of Mohammedans Ordinance. In Zanzibar, on the other hand, Islamic law has been recognized as the "fundamental law" in the courts of His Highness the Sultan, although it has been very widely displaced by statute law in the form of the Sultan's Decrees; but even here provision has been made for the application of a minimum of customary law.

3. The Gambia and Tanganyika

Somewhere between these two categories fall the Gambia in the West and Tanganyika in the East. In the Gambia, the Mohammedan Law Recognition Ordinance, 1905, made provision for the application of Islamic law to Muslims in the Colony of Bathurst in all matters of marriage, divorce, guardianship and succession, while subsequent legislation has set up a second Qāḍī's court, with similar jurisdiction, in the neighboring area of Kombo St. Mary. The Native Tribunal Ordinance, 1933, which provides for the application of native law and custom throughout the Protectorate of the Gambia, also makes specific provision for the application of Islamic law in the Protectorate, in similar matters, where the parties are Muslims. The difference is that in the former courts Islamic law should be applied exclusively (although in reality the customary law, even there, in some respects prevails), while in the latter both the customary law and the Islamic law are officially applicable, and the result is usually a heterogeneous amalgam between the two, compounded according to the knowledge and inclination of the court concerned. And somewhat the same situation obtains in Tanganyika, for here the Islamic law is applied fairly extensively by certain other "local" courts, largely, in practice, as a matter of discretion.[10]

C. Islamic Law Other Than Family Law, Succession, and Waqf

1. East Africa

But what is even more relevant to our present context is to determine to what extent the Islamic law is applied as such outside the basic sphere of family relations and succession or, in East Africa only, the law of waqf.[11] Here the two territories which leap to the mind are Zanzibar in the East and Northern Nigeria in the West. In Zanzibar the position is complicated by the existence of the "dual jurisdiction" of Her Britannic Majesty and His Highness the Sultan; for whereas, under the former

---

[10] Except, that is, within the scope of the Administration (Small Estates) (Amendment) Ordinance and the Asiatics (Marriage, Divorce and Succession) Ordinance, both of 1947.

[11] It is noteworthy that the law of waqf is virtually unknown—in practice—in West Africa.

the Islamic law is applied only in matters of family law, succession and waqf,[12] under the latter the Islamic law, as we have seen, has been proclaimed as the "fundamental law."[13] Even so, this fundamental law has been so extensively displaced by local legislation that only a residuum of Islamic law remains, chiefly in cases of tort,[14] a very limited range of contracts,[15] and questions of real property.[16]

Much the same can be said of the coastal "Protectorate" of Kenya, which is still officially part of the dominions of the Sultan of Zanzibar. The juristic basis for the application of Islamic law in Kenya still goes back, in our view,[17] to the Native Courts Regulations, 1897, where it was provided that "native courts" (a term which at that time included both courts presided over by a European officer and courts presided over by a native authority) should "within the Mohammedan Coast region, or in dealing with Mohammedans, also be guided by, and have regard to, the general principles of the Law of Islam"—as well as being guided by, and having regard to, "any native laws and customs not opposed to natural morality and humanity."[18] But again Islamic law is seldom applied today, even in the Protectorate, outside the law of the family, succession, and waqf, although cases of tort, contract, and real property in which this law is applicable still come before the courts. In the rest of Kenya such cases as occur are almost exclusively governed by the Mohammedan Marriage, Divorce and Succession Ordinance, 1923, or the Waqf Commissioners Ordinance, 1951.[19]

In Tanganyika the juristic basis for the application of Islamic law by the Liwalis and other local courts can, presumably, be found in the fact that parts of this territory were also originally under the jurisdiction of the Sultan of Zanzibar; that the Liwalis continued to apply this law under the German regime; and that the existing law must be regarded as having remained in force under the British administration and since independence, unless and until specifically replaced. Again, however, this means little more in practice than the application of Islamic law to Muslim litigants[20] in matters of family relations, succession, and waqf, although cases of tort, contract, and real property are also, no doubt, sometimes so decided.[21]

---

[12] Under Bombay Regulation 4 of 1827, § 26. This provides for the application—in default of any relevant statute—of the custom of the country, the law of the defendant, or justice, equity and good conscience. This Regulation became applicable to Zanzibar when the legislation of the Bombay Presidency was extended to that country.

[13] *Cf.* Courts Decree, 1923, § 7.

[14] Although few such cases seem, in point of fact, to be heard in the Sultan's courts.

[15] Although the Contract Decree and the Transfer of Property Decree, both of 1917, cover the greater part of the law of contract.

[16] These would fall to be decided according to Islamic law—in default of relevant legislation—even in the British courts, as the *lex loci rei sitae*. But a number of legislative enactments, in fact, cover much of the field. For the law of Zanzibar, see J. N. D. ANDERSON, ISLAMIC LAW IN AFRICA 58-80 (1954).

[17] For a discussion of this controversial question, see *id.* at 82-84.

[18] Native Courts Regulations, 1897, arts. 2 and 3.

[19] For the law of Kenya, see ANDERSON, *op. cit. supra* note 16, at 81-121.

[20] In matters of succession this is governed by the terms of the Administration (Small Estates) (Amendment) Ordinance, 1947, while in the case of immigrant Muslims the Asiatics (Marriage, Divorce and Succession) (Amendment) Ordinance, 1947, applies.

[21] For Tanganyika, see ANDERSON, *op. cit. supra* note 16, at 122-47.

In Uganda, the application of Islamic law is virtually confined to the terms of the Marriage and Divorce of Mohammedans Ordinance, 1906—except, perhaps, for an occasional concession to Muslim influence in the customary law of particular localities.[22] In Nyasaland, again, such concessions appear to be minimal, and Islamic law is not administered as such to any but Asian immigrants under the Asiatics (Marriage, Divorce and Succession) Ordinance, 1929.[23]

In the former British Somaliland Protectorate, on the other hand, Islamic law was everywhere applied in the Qāḍīs' courts in matters of marriage, divorce, succession, waqf, and so on, just as Somali customary law was applicable in other courts in questions of bride-wealth, adultery, insult, and a variety of other matters—on the juristic basis, presumably, that such was the law before the British came. The interrelation of Islamic law and Somali customary law in the life of the Somalis is, indeed, a fascinating study; but it would probably be true to say that outside the limited jurisdiction allotted to the Qāḍīs under the Subordinate Courts Ordinance, 1944, it is the Somali customary law—greatly influenced though this has been, down the centuries, by the law of Islam and of the Arabs—which emerges, in this point or that, from the sphere of family law (in its widest connotation) into the realm of contract, tort, or crime.[24]

2. *West Africa: Northern Nigeria*

When we turn to West Africa, we again find that in the Gambia, Ghana, and Sierra Leone, Islamic law is virtually confined to matters of family relations and succession—whether under the terms of some relevant ordinance[25] or as the "native law and custom" of the area or community concerned. It is only in Nigeria —and there only in the Northern Region[26]—that the law of Islam has been extensively applied in the spheres of criminal law, contract, tort, and procedure. Yet no statutory basis can be found for the application of Islamic law *as such* in Nigeria prior to 1956,[27] other than the comprehensive umbrella of native law and custom. The fact remains, however, that up till 1959 the Islamic law was more extensively applied in Northern Nigeria than anywhere else in the world outside the Arabian peninsula or Afghanistan.

The reason for this phenomenon was, of course, historical. At the inception of the British Protectorate Lord Lugard found many of the Muslim emirates administering justice in a way conspicuously superior to the conditions which prevailed elsewhere; and their courts were not only permitted to continue,[28] but allowed

[22] For Uganda, see *id.* at 148-61.   [23] For Nyasaland, see *id.* at 162-70.
[24] *E.g.*, in regard to the law of *qasāma* or *hāl*. For Somaliland, *cf.* ANDERSON, *op. cit. supra* note 16, at 40-57.
[25] *E.g.*, those mentioned *supra*, at 623-24.
[26] In the Eastern Region there are very few Muslims. And, although there are large numbers of Muslims in the Western Region and in Lagos, they pay scarcely any attention to Islamic law even in the sphere of family relations and succession, where the customary law still prevails.
[27] See *supra* p. 623.
[28] Except that the infliction of punishments such as lapidation and mutilation was forbidden, and that the method of execution was prescribed by law.

to retain the coveted distinction of exercising the "power of life and death"[29]—*i.e.*, trying capital offenses. The result was that jurisdiction, even in homicide cases, was divided between two sets of courts—the "British" and the "native"—each administering a wholly distinct system of law; for in the "British" courts the Nigeria Criminal Code represented a codified form of the common law, while in the Emirs' courts the Islamic law of the Mālikī school prevailed.

As a consequence, a Nigerian who committed a homicide might be tried under the one system or the other,[30] including the appropriate law of evidence and procedure; and the resulting verdict and sentence might depend entirely on this initial circumstance. Not only so, but much might also depend on the religion of the accused and his victim; for in the native courts Muslim witnesses stood on a wholly different footing from non-Muslims, and the blood of a Muslim was regarded as of so much more value than that of an "unbeliever" that the death penalty—which in any case usually depended on the demand of the "heirs of blood"—could seldom be imposed where a Muslim had killed a Christian or a pagan.

This was obviously an impossible position in a country which was on the threshold of independence. It is true that most of the injustices which might have otherwise resulted from this system were in fact averted either on appeal or, more frequently, by the exercise of a British administrative officer's discretion to transfer a case from one court to another at any stage in the proceedings. But it was uncertain how far these safeguards would persist after independence; so the apprehensions of the considerable non-Muslim minority[31] were eminently understandable.

It was in these circumstances that a Panel of Jurists, on which the writer had the honor to serve, was appointed by the Northern Nigerian Government in the summer of 1958. Our terms of reference were to consider, in the light of the legal and judicial systems obtaining in other parts of the world where Muslims and non-Muslims live side by side, whether it was possible to avoid conflicts of law between the three systems of law currently in force in Northern Nigeria (*i.e.*, the English, the Islamic, and the customary law), and to make recommendations as to how this could be done.[32]

To this there was only one possible answer: that such conflicts were minimized in all other mixed communities by the fact that in such localities Islamic law is virtually confined, today, to the personal and family law of Muslim litigants. The major recommendations of the Panel were, therefore, that the Islamic law should be totally excluded from the sphere of criminal justice, whether substantive or procedural, by the promulgation of suitable codes; that it should remain applicable as

---

[29] The only other Commonwealth country in Africa where the courts of an indigenous ruler have such power is Zanzibar; but there the courts of His Highness the Sultan apply the same Penal Decree and are in fact staffed by the self-same judges as the courts of Her Britannic Majesty.

[30] This would, in fact, depend on a number of largely fortuitous circumstances. See Anderson, *Conflict of Laws in North Nigeria: A New Start*, 8 INT'L & COMP. L.Q. 442, 444 (1959).

[31] These are usually reckoned as about one-third of the total population of the Region.

[32] *Cf.* Anderson, *supra* note 30. See also Anderson, *Return Visit to Nigeria: Judicial and Legal Developments in the Northern Region*, 12 INT'L & COMP. L.Q. 282 (1963).

such only in the sphere of family relations and succession, in so far as Muslim litigants were concerned; and that it should also be applicable, where appropriate, either as the law under which some particular contract was in fact concluded or as the law of tort which was locally accepted as valid. And although these recommendations were far more drastic than had been expected—or, indeed, than anyone thought that local opinion would accept—the Northern Nigerian Government not only accepted them in principle but proceeded, in 1959, to give them legislative effect.

This does not mean, of course, that no problems whatever remain in Northern Nigeria today in connection with the law which was formerly so extensively applied. Pressure of Muslim opinion secured the insertion, in the Northern Nigerian Penal Code, of sections penalizing anyone who, being of the Muslim faith, "drinks anything containing alcohol other than for a medicinal purpose"[33] or anyone who, being subject to any native law or custom in which extramarital sexual intercourse is recognized as a criminal offense, indulges in such intercourse with one whom he (or she) knows or has reason to believe is not his (or her) lawful spouse.[34] It is obviously possible that such provisions will be challenged as contrary to section 27 of the Nigeria (Constitution) Order in Council, 1960, which provides that a citizen of Nigeria shall not, by reason of his tribe or religion, be subjected to any law to which citizens of Nigeria from other tribes or religions are not made subject, but with an important proviso.[35]

Again, some confusion seems to prevail at present in regard to cases involving land; for the view that these are governed by customary[36] rather than Islamic law is being increasingly challenged, particularly in matters of inheritance, by the Sharī'a Court of Appeal. Yet again, the provision that the Sharī'a Court of Appeal shall have jurisdiction "where the parties (whether they are Moslems or not) agree in writing that their case shall be dealt with in accordance with Moslem Law"[37] might well lead to confusion if the parties to a case in which the Islamic law was not properly applicable should elect to have their case so decided.

CONCLUSION

If we look at Commonwealth countries in Africa as a whole, it is clear that, today, Islamic law represents a very minor problem outside the sphere of family relations and succession—or, in East Africa, the law of waqf. In the law of contract there can be scant objection to its application, probably to an ever decreasing extent, as the law under which a particular contract was in fact concluded. In the field of tort there is little difficulty in reconciling Islamic concepts with English

[33] Sec. 403.   [34] Secs. 387 and 388.
[35] The Nigerian (Constitution) Order in Council, 1960, § 27(2)(d) provides: "Nothing in this section shall invalidate any law by reason only that the law ... imposes any disability or restriction or accords any privilege or advantage that, having regard to its nature and to special circumstances pertaining to the persons to whom it applies, is reasonably justifiable in a democratic society."
[36] That is, outside the scope of legislative enactments.
[37] Sharī'a Court of Appeal Law, 1959, § 12(e).

principles, and the Islamic law of tort is in fact seldom cited as such today. In matters of land tenure, the major area of conflict is between the English concept of freehold and the customary concept of family or communal rights; and here the Islamic law is closely aligned with the English. For the rest, it is not at all difficult to design legislation acceptable to Muslim opinion to restrain that fragmentation of land holdings which so often results from the unfettered application of the Islamic law of succession. And in the more difficult question of the law of evidence and procedure, experience goes to show that here, too, Muslim opinion is prepared to accept the need to move with the times, at least outside the sphere of family relations.

The first point with which we started this paper largely resolves in practice, therefore, into the question whether a modern society can long remain viable if its legal system enshrines an interpersonal conflict of laws in the sphere of family relations and succession. And to this the answer seems to be an unequivocal affirmative. This is supported by the conclusions of a Conference on the Future of the Law in Africa which met in London in December, 1959, under Lord Denning's chairmanship.[38] It is also confirmed by the experience of such countries as India, Pakistan, Egypt, Lebanon, Syria, and Iraq.

It is undeniable, of course, that a bureaucratic longing for national unity, to say nothing of other pressures, will inevitably—and probably increasingly—inspire a desire for a law of family relations which is applicable to all nationals without distinction of religion; and such, for example, is the avowed objective in the Republic of India. But attempts to translate such a desire into the terms of a draft enactment (as was attempted in a White Paper on Marriage, Divorce, and Inheritance published by the Ghana government in 1961) do not inspire much confidence that this will prove possible—except, of course, at the expense of much offense—unless and until Muslim (and non-Muslim) opinion is prepared to accept a codification which precludes polygamy, severely restricts divorce, and abrogates the rule that there can be no inheritance between those who differ in religion.[39] A desire for national unity was indeed one of the chief motives behind the promulgation of the Iraqi Code of Personal Status, 1959; but it is noteworthy that this code made no attempt to do more than unify the law applicable to Sunnīs and Shī'īs, respectively, and that in the matter of intestate succession even this limited objective was achieved only by the drastic expedient of completely abandoning the Islamic law in favor of the statute law previously applicable to government land.[40]

This brings us to the second question with which we started this paper, but again

---

[38] THE LONDON CONFERENCE ON THE FUTURE OF LAW IN AFRICA, RECORD OF THE PROCEEDINGS. (Allott ed. 1960). See 4 J. AFRICAN LAW 1 (1960).

[39] As, for example, in Turkey, where the family law of Switzerland was taken over almost in toto in 1926; but a much less drastic example can also be found in the Tunisian Code of Personal Law, 1956 and 1959. It is noteworthy, however, that the Ghana White Paper, quite contrary to the current tendency in the Arab world, favored giving statutory recognition to the unrestricted polygamy of the customary law—even in the case of Christians and Muslims—although only one wife could be actually registered as such.

[40] See Anderson, *A Law of Personal Status for Iraq,* 9 INT'L & COMP. L.Q. 542 (1960).

with a drastic limitation in its scope. Instead of asking whether an authoritative law, which is regarded as firmly based on divine revelation, can so adapt itself—or be adapted—as to enable it to resolve the typical conflicts of an industrial society, we must in fact pose the question whether this law can so adapt itself, or be adapted, as to enable it to conform to contemporary ideas of marriage, divorce, and succession. And the answer which comes from some of the more progressive Muslim countries seems here, again, to represent at least a qualified affirmative.

We have already seen how the Islamic law has been quietly put on one side in these countries almost completely in the sphere of criminal and commercial law, the law of evidence and procedure, and the greater part of the contents of the civil codes. In the sphere of family law and succession, on the other hand, no Muslim country other than Turkey has gone so far as this.[41] Instead, Muslim countries have contrived to effect reforms in what purports (at least) to be still Islamic law by a variety of ingenious devices. One is a procedural device, by which parts of the Islamic law are simply precluded from judicial enforcement (or even recognition). Another, which has been given the widest possible application, consists in an eclectic selection of principles for which some support can be found among the heterogeneous Muslim authorities of the past, and the promulgation of these principles in the form of statute law. Yet another, which has received much less acknowledgment, represents a reinterpretation of the ancient texts in a manner more acceptable to contemporary opinion. And each of these is at times reinforced by statutory regulations which are represented as augmenting, rather than contradicting, the sacred law.[42]

By such devices the twin evils of child marriage and compulsory marriage have been largely remedied[43] in the Arab world, although they still represent a considerable problem in some of the Commonwealth countries in East and West Africa. Polygamy, too, has been somewhat restricted in Syria, still more circumscribed in Morocco and Iraq, and completely forbidden in Tunisia. By the same means ill-used wives have been given the right to a judicial dissolution of marriage in those countries in which the ascendancy of the dominant Ḥanafī doctrine previously excluded any such relief. But the restriction of a husband's unfettered right to repudiate his wife at his unilateral discretion has proved far more difficult. Only in Tunisia[44] has it been unequivocally enacted that a divorce pronounced outside a court of law will have no legal effect—and, even so, there is nothing to prevent a husband (or, indeed, in Tunisia a wife) from insisting on a divorce, provided he (or she) is willing to pay the financial compensation which the court may decree in favor of the injured party.[45]

[41] Except for Iraq, in so far as the law of intestate succession is concerned.
[42] *Cf.* J. N. D. ANDERSON, ISLAMIC LAW IN THE MODERN WORLD (1959), and numerous articles on this subject.
[43] In so far, that is, as this can be achieved by legislative enactments.
[44] Followed, but not quite so unequivocally, by Iraq.
[45] *Cf.* in this context, Anderson, *The Tunisian Law of Personal Status*, 7 INT'L & COMP. L.Q. 262, 267 (1958), and Anderson, *The Modernization of Islamic Law in the Sudan*, 5 SUDAN L.J. AND REPORTS 306 *ff.* (1960).

This is not the place to discuss how far these reforms are based on principles which can be claimed as genuinely Islamic, or whether they must be acknowledged as not only inspired but actually borrowed from the West. It is sufficient for our present purpose that they have in fact been effected in Muslim countries and are proving, with the passage of time, ever more acceptable to Muslim opinion. Setbacks may of course occur in one country or another; but it seems overwhelmingly probable that similar reforms, at least on a limited scale, will before long extend to the countries of East and West Africa, and will little by little prepare the ground for what may one day represent a unification of the family law. There can be no doubt that such a unification would solve many problems—particularly, perhaps, in those areas where individuals frequently change their religion, or where persons of different religions intermarry.[46] For the present, however, any such development seems sufficiently remote; and it can scarcely be maintained that an interpersonal conflict of laws, if confined to such matters as marriage, divorce, and succession, represents any major barrier to national advance.

[46] In such cases difficult problems regarding the law of inheritance which is properly applicable, or even regarding the validity of a marriage, today frequently occur. *Cf.* ANDERSON, *op. cit. supra* note 16, at 110-18, 125-28, 137, 144-46, 216.

UNITED NATIONS LAW IN AFRICA: THE CONGO OPERATION AS A CASE STUDY

Thomas M. Franck*

Introduction

The United Nations Operation in the Congo (ONUC) is not a mutant: its pedigree boasts such formidable progenitors as the Korean Unified Command, the Palestine Truce Supervisory Organization, the United Nations Middle East Emergency Force (UNEF), and the Laos Peace Observer Group.

The common gene which united ONUC with these others is *interposition*: the injection of a United Nations presence to bring international law to bear in a situation of international chaos. ONUC also combines in itself other selected characteristics of its predecessors. It has inherited from UNEF the concept of an internationally-recruited military contingent; from the Korean Command, ONUC has taken the element of mandatory decisions backed by force. The Lebanon Observation Group bequeathed it the nature of a neutral intervention.

In combining these various elements, ONUC has created for itself a unique personality: it is by far the most ambitious interposition to date in a situation characterized by haphazard decolonization, tribal warfare, and cold war pressures. A brief glance at the principal remaining "colonial" areas of Africa—Angola, Mozambique, South Africa, and Southern Rhodesia—unfortunately does not induce the comforting thought that this uniqueness will be perpetual.

Should the need arise again in any of these other "colonial" areas would the world turn once more to the United Nations? The answer, in part weighted by fear of the alternatives, will largely depend on the assessment the world, and particularly the African states themselves, make of the role played by the United Nations in the Congo.

Since ONUC has been carefully and constantly governed by expressed law, and since it has by its deliberate choice and application of precedent and its recourse to reasoned innovation also *made* law, a fair assessment of its impact on the Congo must be weighed not only on the scale of politics but also of law.

I

Legal Basis for the United Nations Presence

Even while the ritual jollifications of independence were still under way, the tender plant of national responsibility was being trampled underfoot by inexperienced and undisciplined elements in the new state. King Baudouin proclaimed the Congo

* B.A. 1952, LL.B. 1953, University of British Columbia; LL.M. 1954, S.J.D. 1959, Harvard University. Professor of Law, New York University. Author, Race and Nationalism—The Struggle for Power in Rhodesia-Nyasaland (1960).

independent on Thursday, June 30, 1960. Exactly two weeks thereafter, the United Nations Security Council had already passed its first Congo resolution; and thirty-six hours later, the first of the ONUC contingents began taking up positions under the Blue and White flag.

Violence had broken out on July 2 in the vicinities of Léopoldville and Luluabourg, and three days later the mutiny of the Congolese army (the ANC) was in full cry. Of all the components of Congolese self-government, the ANC was the most precarious link in an ill-forged chain. Discipline was harsh, pay low, and—since no Congolese had ever been commissioned—incentives were utterly lacking. The predominantly Flemish command made as scant effort to hide their scorn for the Congolese as for the Belgian politicians. Yet the pre-emptory discharge of all Belgian officers on July 8 had the explosive effect of suddenly lifting the lid from an overheated pressure cooker. As the rampaging army both provoked and then forcibly halted the flight of thousands of whites, Belgian troops began to fan out from their two bases of Kamina and Kitona, and additional paratroopers were brought in by air.

In the context of the confusion which prevailed in the Congo during July, it would be surprising if the legal image of Belgian intervention were to emerge clearly. In the retrospective opinion of the present Government of the Congo, "only the Minister of Defense, at that time Mr. Patrice Lumumba, had the authority, by virtue of the Belgian-Congolese General Treaty of Friendship, Assistance and Cooperation, to make an appeal for the military intervention of the Belgian troops."[1]

No such appeal was made. M. Lumumba did, at one point, it appears, "agree in principle that the Belgian metropolitan troops operating in Luluabourg can remain for at least two months . . ."[2] but only under certain conditions. Moreover, the agreement—if it were such—did not cover the more extensive Belgian interventions at Elizabethville[3] and elsewhere. Indeed, the Congolese Government on the very same day requested United States troops to counteract the Belgian intervention.[4] When this direct assistance was refused, they turned to the United Nations in accordance with the suggestion that accompanied the United States rejection.

In a communication addressed to the Secretary General on July 12, 1960, President Kasavubu and Prime Minister Lumumba requested the "dispatch by the United Nations of military assistance . . . to protect the national territory of the Congo against the present external aggression which is a threat to world peace," an element

[1] REPUBLIC OF THE CONGO, MINISTRY OF FOREIGN AFFAIRS, DOCUMENT DIVISION, THE PROVINCE OF THE KATANGA AND CONGOLESE INDEPENDENCE 17 (1962). The treaty was never ratified by the Congolese Chambers and was later denounced by the Government of the Congo.
[2] Letter from M. Lumumba to the Belgian Consul General in Luluabourg, July 11, 1960, *id.* at 17-18.
[3] Katanga had, on July 11, proclaimed its secession, and M. Tshombe, as its Prime Minister, had not only requested but demanded the dispatch of Belgian troops to Elizabethville. *Id.* at 18-21.
[4] Interview with Dr. Oscar Schachter, legal counsel to the U.N. Acting Secretary-General, New York, N.Y., April 30, 1962.

of which is "a conspiracy between Belgian imperialists and a small group of Katanga leaders" to perpetrate "the secession of Katanga . . . which means the disguised perpetuation of colonialist regime."[5]

The Congolese complaint contains three distinct elements:

    a) an allegation of external aggression,
    b) an allegation of a conspiracy to bring about the secession of Katanga,
    c) a request for United Nations military aid to bring an end to both these alleged infractions of Congolese sovereignty.

As a "party to a dispute" the Congo could, even though it was not at the time a member of the United Nations,[6] itself bring a complaint before the Security Council under terms of article 35(2) of the Charter. In choosing not to do so, the Congo instead requested the Secretary General to proceed for the first time on his own initiative under article ninety-nine, whereby he "may bring to the attention of the Security Council any matter which in his opinion may threaten the maintenance of international peace and security." This obviated a jurisdictional decision as to whether a "dispute" or "situation" existed since his mere *belief* to that effect is sufficient to create initial jurisdiction.

On July 13, 1960, therefore, the Secretary General circulated the following memorandum:[7]

I wish to inform you that I have to bring to the attention of the Security Council a matter which, in my opinion, may threaten the maintenance of international peace and security. Thus, I request you to call an urgent meeting of the Security Council to hear a report of the Secretary-General on a demand for United Nations action in relation to the Republic of the Congo.

May I suggest that the meeting is called for tonight at 8:30 p.m.

That evening, the Secretary General outlined to the hurriedly convened Security Council the framework of a proposed United Nations intervention. His efforts were spurred by a further communication from the Congolese President and Prime Minister threatening that if military assistance was not received without delay, the Republic of the Congo would be obliged to appeal to the Bandung Treaty Powers[8]— a euphemism for Chinese "volunteers." The Secretary General's charge to the Council classified the presence of Belgian troops in the Congo as "a source of internal,

---

[5] U.N. SECURITY COUNCIL OFF. REC. 15th year, Supp. July-Sept. 1960, at 11 (S/4382) (1960).
[6] United Nations membership had been requested on July 1, by Prime Minister Lumumba (U.N. Doc. No. S/4361) and had received immediate Security Council approval (U.N. Doc. No. S/4377). However, the General Assembly did not act on the application until it met in the fall. Resolutions of the Fifteenth Session, Vol. 2, U.N. Doc. No. 1480 (XV), Admission of the Republic of the Congo (Léopoldville) to Membership in the United Nations (Item 20), Doc. A/L 599, Sept. 20, 1960, U.N. GEN. Ass. OFF. REC. 15th sess., Supp. No. 16 (A/4684) at 64 (1960).
[7] U.N. Doc. No. S/4381.
[8] Annual Report of the Secretary General on the Work of the Organization, June 16, 1960-June 16, 1961, U.N. GEN. Ass. OFF. REC. 16th Sess., Supp. No. 1, at 1 (A/4800) (1961) [hereinafter cited as ANNUAL REPORT]. See also U.N. Doc. No. S/4382, at 2.

and potentially also of international tension" and urged their replacement by "technical assistance of a military nature."[9]

The earnest discussion continued through the night. Early on Thursday morning the Security Council adopted a resolution introduced by Tunisia but generally reflecting the Secretary General's views.[10] No negative votes were cast, but China, France, and the United Kingdom abstained out of deference to the views of Belgium.[11]

In his appearance before the Security Council the Secretary General had suggested the following: (1) the dispatch of a military force; (2) the standards for its formation; (3) the limitations on its function. The most important elements of (3) were that the proposed force not be allowed to act in any way likely to make it a party to internal conflicts or to use force except in self-defense.[12]

The July 14 resolution of the Security Council incorporates both the Kasavubu-Lumumba request of July 12 and the Secretary General's appeal of July 13 in its terms,[13] and, in the words of the Secretary General, his statement to the Council "may be regarded as a basic document on the interpretation of the mandate."[14] Yet that statement is not entirely reconcilable with the Kasavubu-Lumumba request, for the latter distinctly invites help against the "conspiracy between Belgian imperialists and a small group of Katangese leaders" while the former excludes the use of force in anything but self-defense and abjures all intervention in domestic disputes.

This latent contradiction was not at first apparent. The Secretary General, in postulating the principle of "neutral" intervention, proceeded in accordance with the working principles he had formulated for the Lebanon Observation Group in 1958.[15] In the Lebanon case, United Nations removal of "outside" intervention (by the United States and infiltrators from neighboring states) had been sufficient to retire that case from the list of active "situations." In the Congo, this happy consequence was similarly expected to follow: the removal of Belgian and other foreign intervention was expected to end the danger of the "Katanga conspiracy" and civil war. In fact, however, it did not; and when it became apparent very soon that some of the deepest roots of the Congo crisis were sunk in purely Congolese soil, and that

[9] ANNUAL REPORT 1. See also U.N. SECURITY COUNCIL OFF. REC. 15th year, 873d meeting 11-12 (S/PV. 873) (1960).
[10] U.N. Doc. No. S/4387. Resolution as submitted by Tunisia, S/4383, adopted July 13, 1960 (same text as S/4387).
[11] ANNUAL REPORT 2.   [12] *Id.* at 1.
[13] "The Security Council, considering the report of the Secretary-General on a request for the United Nations action in relation to the Republic of the Congo, considering the request for military assistance addressed to the Secretary-General by the President and the Prime Minister of the Republic of the Congo . . . ."
[14] First Report by the Secretary-General on the Implementation of the Security Council Resolution of July 14, 1960 (S/4387) at 1, U.N. SECURITY COUNCIL OFF. REC. 15th year, Supp. July-Sept. 1960, at 16 (S/4389 and Add. 1-6 (1960) [hereinafter cited as FIRST REPORT].
[15] See Annual Report of the Secretary-General on the Work of the Organization, June 16, 1958-June 15, 1959, U.N. GEN. ASS. OFF. REC. 15th Sess., Supp. No. 1, at 15-22 (A/4132) (1959).

they were yet sufficient to sustain a sinister tree that cast an international shadow, the dichotomy between "help against internal conspiracy" and "neutrality in internal conflicts" became an acute problem for the United Nations.

Nor did the terms of the July 14 resolution[16] help to clarify matters. Besides incorporating the Kasavubu-Lumumba and Hammarskjold submissions, it did two things: (1) called on Belgian troops to withdraw, and (2) authorized *military assistance to the Government of the Congo in consultation with that Government until in the opinion of that Government its forces were able to meet the task of preserving national security.*

What was the United Nations' role: *neutrality* or *the active rendering of military assistance to the Government of the Congo to preserve national security against secessionists?* The problem was barely discernible on July 14, although Katanga had proclaimed its independence already on July 11.[17]

The vagueness of the resolution of July 14, 1960, and the subsequent mandates of the Security Council, which in the words of the President of the General Assembly imposed "an intolerable burden of interpretation and discretion" on the Secretary-General, are due to a number of factors. Were these resolutions subject to the stringent test of the *Schechter* case,[18] they would almost certainly be void for vagueness. Yet such sweeping delegation is scarcely the unique experience of the Congo Operation. When the General Assembly some four years earlier decided to establish the United Nations Emergency Force (UNEF), it was by an even more standard-less mandate to the Secretary-General. The resolution of November 2, 1956,[19]

> ... requests, as a matter of priority, [the Secretary-General] to submit ... within 48 hours a plan for the setting up, with the consent of the nations concerned, of an emergency international United Nations Force to secure and supervise the cessation of hostilities in accordance with all the terms of the aforementioned resolution.

The same resolution also "authorizes the Secretary-General immediately to arrange with the parties concerned for the implementation of the cease-fire and the halting of the movement of military forces and arms into the area . . ." and "to obtain compliance of the withdrawal of all forces behind the armistice lines."[20] How was the Emergency Force to be set up? What was to be the standard and rate of withdrawal? What points of interposition (such as that at Shaarm el Shiek on the Gulf of Akaba) were the United Nations to occupy? It was all left for the Secretary-General to determine.

[16] U.N. Doc. No. S/4383.
[17] For a discussion of the domestic constitutionality of this act see THE PROVINCE OF KATANGA AND CONGOLESE INDEPENDENCE, *op. cit. supra* note 1, at 18-22. See also the discussion of articles 110 and 114 of the Loi Fondamentale in the light of political events contained in THOMAS M. FRANCK & JOHN CAREY, THE ROLE OF THE UNITED NATIONS IN THE CONGO—A RETROSPECTIVE PERSPECTIVE (1962).
[18] Schechter Poultry Corp. v. United States, 295 U.S. 495 (1935).
[19] Resolution 998, GEN. ASS. OFF. REC. 1st Emergency Special Sess., Supp. No. 1, at 2 (A/3354) (1956).
[20] Resolution 999, *ibid.*

What are the causes of this vagueness? Certainly it is not a matter of bad drafting, although resolutions do sometimes reflect the haste in which they are born. More important is an element equally responsible for vagueness in congressional enactments: the expediency of compromise.

Immediately after the vote on the July 14 resolution, the Soviet Union and Poland announced that they had voted for the text because its principal object was to effect the immediate withdrawal of the Belgians. The United States declared that it had voted for the resolution because it made provision for technical assistance to law and order but that they doubted the wisdom of calling for Belgian withdrawal. In implementing the resolution, the United States stated, the Secretary General "must not . . . contribute to the perpetuation of public disorder by insisting upon the withdrawal of military units capable of assisting in the protection of life and property without the establishment of other methods to accomplish that task"—a direct contradiction of the Soviet interpretation that at once presented a dilemma to the Secretary-General[21] which could not be papered over by reference to the vague text of the resolution itself.

Yet vagueness of language may be the only way to get action at all: a word formula deferring the really difficult decisions to the course of events and the discretion of the administrators. In many instances this is a good thing. As in the regulation of new domestic problems—the allocation of television channels, for example—a more vaguely delegated standard of administration may be necessary to allow room for *ad hoc* solutions to unpredictable problems. Vague delegation may also be useful in shifting to anonymous administrative officials the task of making decisions generally regarded as necessary but for which some or all of the Powers do not, for political reasons, wish to take responsibility.

In this way, broad delegation helps break log jams. But it may also allow the logs to move too quickly. States may, in fact, vigorously oppose a course of action on which the Secretariat has already embarked in the honest belief that it is acting within the scope of the delegated authority. Worse, states may hypocritically support a popular resolution with their public vote while at the same time sabotaging its execution by subterfuge in the field or in the accounting office. There are, obviously, dangers inherent in action carried out in accordance with a legal mandate that creates the illusion of agreement where none in fact exists. In the understated words of the Secretary General,[22]

The character of the mandates has in many cases been such that in carrying out his functions the Secretary-General has found himself forced also to interpret the decisions in the light of the Charter, United Nations precedent and the aims and intentions expressed by the members. . . . Developments have sometimes led to situations in which he has had to shoulder responsibilities for certain limited political functions.

[21] ANNUAL REPORT 2.
[22] Introduction to the Annual Report of the Secretary-General on the Work of the Organization, June 16, 1960-June 15, 1961, U.N. GEN. Ass. OFF. REC. 16th Sess., Supp. No. 1A (A/4800/Add.1) (1961).

It is against this initial vagueness, compounded by later resolutions, that all legal aspects of the United Nations interposition in the Congo must be assessed.

II
United Nations Jurisdiction in the Congo: Contract or Legislation?

The previous international military action of the United Nation, UNEF, was in many ways similar to the ONUC operation. Like the Congo undertaking, UNEF was set up on a temporary emergency basis, with "no intent in the establishment of the force to influence the ... political balance...."[23] In creating the Congo force, the Secretary General was able to lean heavily on the experience of the earlier action.[24]

There was, however, one clear legal difference between the inception of UNEF and that of ONUC. According to the Secretary General, UNEF functioned "on the basis of a decision reached under the terms of the resolution 'Uniting for Peace,'" and being a creation of the General Assembly, which only has the power to make recommendations, it was,[25]

limited in its operation to the extent that consent of the parties concerned is required under generally recognized international law. While the General Assembly is enabled to *establish* the force with the consent of those parties which contribute units to the force, it could not request for force to be *stationed* or *operate* on the territory of a given country without the consent of the Government of that country.

This consensual or contractual element was fundamental to the UNEF presence in Egypt. When it came to recruiting national contingents, "Egypt had what amounted to a veto power."[26] This was demonstrated, for example, by Egypt's rejection of the Queen's Own Rifles of Canada.[27] Moreover, Egyptian consent to the landing of the force had to be specifically communicated by telegram on November 14[28] before the first troops disembarked.

ONUC was a different breed altogether. Its authorization rested not on the General Assembly's recommendatory powers but on chapter seven of the United

---

[23] Second and Final Report of the Secretary General on the Plan for an Emergency International United Nations Force, U.N. Gen. Ass. Off. Rec. 1st Emergency Spec. Sess. Annexes, Agenda Item No. 5, at 19 (A/3302 and Adds. 1-30) (1956).

[24] There were, however, some important refinements. The UNEF contingent was recruited on the principle of universality but exclusion of nationals of the Big Five powers. The Secretary-General even "politely rebuffed a British-French effort to take part in deciding the composition of the staff and contingents." W. Frye, A United Nations Peace Force 11 (1957). See also Second and Final Report of the Secretary-General, *supra* note 23, at 4; and Resolution 1000, U.N. Gen. Ass. Off. Rec. 1st Emergency Spec. Sess., Supp. No. 1, at 2 (A/3354) (1956), which specifically excludes recruitment of officers or troops from "the permanent members of the Security Council." The same principle was followed in organizing ONUC with the significant added qualifications that the contingent would not include units "from any country which, because of its geographical position or for other reasons, might be considered as possibly having a special interest in the situation...." Annual Report 2.

[25] Second and Final Report of the Secretary-General, *supra* note 23, at 4.

[26] Frye, *op. cit. supra* note 24, at 16.   [27] *Id.* at 23-31.

[28] Report of the Secretary-General on Basic Points for the Presence and Functioning in Egypt of the United Nations Emergency Force, Nov. 20, 1956, U.N. Gen. Ass. Off. Rec. 11th Sess., Annexes, Agenda Item No. 66, at 9 (A/3375 and Annex Aide-Memoire) (1956).

Nations Charter, which defines powers of the Security Council as regards "threats to the peace, breaches of the peace, and acts of aggression." Decisions taken by the Security Council are not mere recommendations; they are compulsory mandates which the members of the United Nations "agree to accept and carry out."[29] If the Congo was not under this obligation in July, it clearly has been since its admission to membership in September, 1960. *Its adherence to the decisions of the Security Council is therefore not based on contract but upon legislation.* This makes an important difference: (1) a legislative intervention can be altered legislatively, while a contract can only be altered by the consent of the parties; and (2) a legislative intervention cannot be terminated as a consensual relationship might, by the withdrawal of the host country's consent.[30]

The practical differences between the two relationships are readily apparent. The United Nations went into the Congo to provide technical assistance in consultation with the Congolese Government. But, unlike UNEF, it was not there on sufferance. Right from its inception, "the Organization reserved for itself the authority to decide on the composition of the Force" although it "should take fully into account the view of the host Government."[31] Moreover,

although the United Nations Force under the resolution is dispatched to the Congo at the request of the Government and will be present in the Congo with its consent, and although it may be considered as serving as an arm of the Government for the maintenance of order and protection of life—tasks which naturally belong to the national authorities and which will pass to such authorities as soon as, in the view of the Government, they are sufficiently firmly established—the Force is necessarily under the exclusive command of the United Nations. . . . The Force is thus not under the orders of the Government nor can it . . . be permitted to become a party to any internal conflict.

Further, because the Congo is obliged "when exercising its sovereign right with regard to the presence of the Force [to] be guided by good faith in the interpretation of the purposes of the Force," it follows (as a matter of right, not of agreement) that

the United Nations activity should have freedom of movement within its area of operations and all such facilities regarding access to that area and communications as are necessary for a successful accomplishment of the task.[32]

[29] U.N. CHARTER art. 25. It is not clear just which articles of the Charter constitute the authority for the Security Council's action. However, the International Court has recently held that "the operations known as UNEF and ONUC were not *enforcement* actions within the compass of Chapter VII . . . ." Certain Expenses of the United Nations (U.N. CHARTER art. 17, para. 2), Advisory Opinion of 20 July 1962: [1962] I.C.J. Rep. 157, 166. Thus the Security Council must be deemed to have acted under article 40, which is in chapter VII but is not an enforcement measure, being more in the nature of an interlocutory order.

[30] Even Egypt, however, in its "contract" with the United Nations agreed, however vaguely, that "the United Nations understanding this to correspond to the wishes of the Government of Egypt, reaffirms its willingness to maintain the UNEF until its task is completed."

[31] ANNUAL REPORT 2. "While it is for the United Nations alone to decide on the composition of military elements sent to a country, the United Nations should, in deciding on composition, take fully into account the viewpoint of the host Government as one of the most serious factors which should guide the recruitment of personnel." U.N. Doc. No. S/4389, at 4.

[32] U.N. Doc. No. S/4389, at 3.

A general agreement with the Congolese authorities was in fact obtained, but only some days *after* troops had begun to land, and it was needed, according to the United Nations, not for jurisdiction, but for the more limited purpose of "specifying what is to be considered the area of operations."[33] Even before any such specifications were agreed upon, the United Nations had already placed Ndjili airfield at Léopoldville under United Nations control, assuming all responsibility for military, administrative, and transport staffing of its facilities.[34]

At no time during the formation of the United Nations Force or thereafter were the United Nations obliged to act as if the ONUC operation were a consensual undertaking cut to the pattern of UNEF. Quite the contrary. When the Congolese Government demanded the withdrawal of Ghanaian troops, they were rebuffed. When the Central Government demanded to be associated with the United Nations entry into Elizabethville, the Secretary General

informed the Congolese Prime Minister of the resolution adopted that day by the (Security) Council and drew his attention to the fact that it was mandatory, in particular where, on the basis of Article 49 of the Charter, it requested the cooperation of all Member States....

He also informed President Kasavubu "that there could be no question of conditions as of an agreement on that matter...."[35] Similarly, when President Kasavubu, on January 7 and 14, 1961 requested the recall of the United Nations Special Representative, Ambassador Dayal, who was in field command of the entire ONUC, the Secretary General drew attention to the fact that "the Special Representative was not a diplomatic representative accredited to the Congolese Government but a senior official of the Secretariat" and that it was "impossible . . . to accede to the demand...."[36] In several important instances, also, the Secretary General authorized the use of force against the Government of the Congo—once to protect the territorial immunity of the Ghanaian Embassy in Léopoldville[37] and once to defend ONUC's exclusive control of the key port of Matadi.[38] The United Nations also cordoned off certain areas in Léopoldville, Stanleyville, Bukavu, Goma, and in other parts of Kivu, Kasai, and Katanga as "neutral zones" for political refugees, without obtaining the prior consent—indeed, over the objections—of the Congo Government.[39]

---

[33] *Ibid.* For text of the preliminary agreement, see U.N. Doc. No. S/4389/Add.5. The text of the final agreement of Nov. 27, 1961 is contained in U.N. Doc. Nos. S/5004 and A/4986.
[34] U.N. Doc. No. S/4389/Add.1.
[35] ANNUAL REPORT 7. [36] *Id.* at 33.
[37] On Nov. 15, 1960, M. Lovelace Mensah, third secretary of the Ghanaian Embassy in Léopoldville, was arrested by Colonel Mobutu's troops. He had allegedly been carrying funds to M. Lumumba—an allegation denied by the Ghanaians. An expulsion order was issued to Mr. Nathaniel Welbeck, the Ghanaian charge d'affaires, but was ignored. After waiting three days, the Congolese troops set upon the Embassy around which ONUC troops had been posted. Both Mr. Hammarskjold and Mr. Bunche agreed with Mr. Dayal to uphold the doctrine of inviolability of embassies as against the doctrine of *persona non grata*. Four Congolese, including the deputy chief of staff, were killed in the engagement. See ANNUAL REPORT 14.
[38] The Matadi incidents and similar efforts by Central Government troops to oust the United Nations from control of Ndjili airfield and other key installations is discussed in ANNUAL REPORT 37-39.
[39] ANNUAL REPORT 37-38.

The implications of a mandatory, nonconsensual United Nations action of the ONUC stripe are far more important than the scattered incidents which attest to its mandatory nature. It is most important, for example, that the ONUC Operation may—as indeed from the very beginning, we have observed, it did—depart from the terms of the inceptive request of the host country. These departures and innovations mounted as the nature of the political crisis changed, and the consent of the Congolese authorities was never regarded, by any member of the United Nations with the possible exception of France, as a prerequisite to altering the nature of the intervention. Thus, the second Security Resolution, that of July 22, 1960, for the first time impliedly authorized the ONUC to restore "law and order in the Republic of the Congo"[40]—and without further caveat about acting "in consultation with the Government of the Congo." As late as August 9, the Security Council still reaffirmed that "the United Nations Force in the Congo will not be a party to, or in any way intervene in or be used to influence the outcome of any internal conflict."[41]

This policy of *laissez faire* towards the civil war was based on the illusion that once the Belgians left of their own accord, the crisis would be over, an illusion captured in the Secretary General's instructions to ONUC troops: ". . . [M]en engaged in the operation may never take the initiative in the use of armed force, but are [only] entitled to respond with force to an attack with arms. . . ."[42] It was under those terms that the United Nations entered both the Congo and, on August 12, the "independent state" of Katanga. Just prior to the August landing in Elizabethville the Secretary General also reiterated that the resolution of August 9, instructing ONUC to enter Katanga, did not authorize it "to intervene with armed troops in an internal conflict. . . ."[43] Yet, on February 21, 1961, the Security Council reacted to the changed circumstances of M. Lumumba's murder by authorizing the United Nations to "use force, if necessary, in the last resort [to] prevent the occurrence of civil war" and bring about "the halting of all military operations."[44] It also impliedly authorized ONUC to promote certain objectives strongly resisted by the Central Government, such as the "convening of the Parliament" and the reorganization of the army (ANC).[45]

An equally radical departure is the authorization,[46] in the Security Council resolution of November 24, 1961, for

the Secretary-General to take vigorous action, including the use of a requisite measure of force, if necessary, for the immediate apprehension, detention pending legal action and/or deportation of all foreign military and para-military personnel and political advisers not under United Nations Command. . . .

Although this was the first specific authority for the use of force against foreign political advisers, it was not by any means the beginning of the United Nations

[40] U.N. Doc. No. S/4405.
[41] U.N. Doc. No. S/4424.
[42] U.N. Doc. No. S/4389 at 5.
[43] U.N. Doc. No. S/PV.887 at 17.
[44] U.N. Doc. No. S/4741.
[45] *Ibid.* See also ANNUAL REPORT 38.
[46] U.N. Doc. No. S/5002. For Congolese Government opposition to this, see ANNUAL REPORT 38.

campaign to eliminate this non-military influence from the Government of Katanga and from the Central Government.

In his report of November 2, 1960, Special Representative Dayal had already sighted the conflict between ONUC and the Belgian political advisers—men, generally, of undersecretarial or *chefs de cabinet* rank who had returned in large numbers after the first wave of terror had receded.[47] "As a result," Ambassador Dayal complained,[48]

> the task of ONUC has been made more difficult . . . cooperation with ONUC, vital to its smooth functioning, has been hampered in various ways by high-ranking Belgians. United Nations documents and reports have frequently been withheld from the Congolese officials in the ministries and propaganda has been engineered regarding the supposed dangers of the emergence of United Nations trusteeship. . . .
> The motives and activities of a significant portion of these returning officials appears to be clearly at variance with the principles of the General Assembly resolution and the ONUC's basic objectives.[49]

It was not, however, until the death of Patrice Lumumba with which, rightly or wrongly, Belgian advisers were popularly associated[50] that the Security Council for the first time urged "the immediate withdrawal of and evacuation from the Congo of all Belgian and other . . . political advisers not under the United Nations Command."[51]

The Central Government of the Congo was little more pleased than the Government of Katanga[52] by these new departures in United Nations policy. Nevertheless, on April 17, 1961, President Kasavubu reluctantly signed an "agreement in principle" with the Secretary-General acquiescing in "the elimination of all deleterious foreign influences" in the Central Government and also to United Nations-assisted reorganization of the ANC.[53] Neither provision has ever been completely implemented although pressure in that direction is still being exerted.

In these important matters the United Nations can alter, and in practice has unilaterally altered, the original terms of its Congo intervention (if "unilateral" is a word to describe the actions of more than 100 nations acting in concert). It also follows that nothing short of a decision to do so by the Organization can bring the intervention to an end. This despite the terms of the original resolution[54] to the effect that United Nations intervention will continue only until "the national security forces may be able, *in the opinion of the Government,* to meet fully their

---

[47] The Belgian population of the Congo which had fallen from 100,000 to 20,000 in the autumn, had again doubled by February 1961. The Times (London) Feb. 24, 1961; The Observer, Feb. 19, 1961.
[48] Second Progress Report to the Secretary-General of his Special Representative, Nov. 2, 1960, U.N. Doc. No. S/4557 at 16-18.
[49] *Id.* art. 9.
[50] See Report of the Commission of Investigation Established Under the Terms of General Assembly Resolution 1601 (XV), Nov. 11, 1960, U.N. Doc. Nos. A/4964 and S/4976.
[51] Resolution of Feb. 21, 1961, U.N. Doc. No. S/4741.
[52] ANNUAL REPORT 37-41.   [53] *Id.* at 39.
[54] U.N. Doc. No. S/4387. (Emphasis added.)

tasks." In fact, of course, and despite occasioned rough passage in the relations between the ONUC and the Congo, no such request has ever been made by the Central Government.

Indeed, during the political interregnum between Premiers Lumumba and Adoula it is doubtful that there was a government competent to make such a request. The fact, in either case, remains that the ONUC, although it incorporated the Congolese request in its initial enabling resolution, is an exercise of United Nations jurisdiction under chapter seven of the Charter, which is not subject to termination at the request of the host state. This, again, was not true of UNEF, and UNEF's agreement with Egypt deliberately left unclear the question of "winding-up."[55] The ONUC agreement, however, is quite specific:[56]

The United Nations reaffirms, considering it to be in accordance with the wishes of the Government of the Republic of the Congo, that it is prepared to maintain the United Nations Force in the Congo until such time as *it* deems the latter's task to have been fully accomplished.

The pronoun "it" obviously refers solely to the United Nations.

It is therefore apparent that a nation which invites the United Nations to participate in a play on its stage, cannot by itself ring down the curtain. It cannot bind the legislative power of the Organization to a particular method or duration of intervention. In such a situation, the United Nations intervenes as of right. By assisting or requesting the intervention the host-state may gain bargaining leverage in its day-to-day relations with an administration which will travel far to achieve its given objectives by peaceful cooperation—but it cannot alter the legal status of the intervention.

Yet these legalities may be somewhat misleading. It is true in law that the United Nations intervened on the basis of its Charter powers and not, as in UNEF, on the basis of the request or consent of the host-state. On the other hand, it is equally true that in practice, an intervention such as that of ONUC would probably never have occurred had the Congo not issued an invitation. Aside from the logistic difficulties of intervening in opposition to the host state, there is the great political unlikelihood of enlisting Afro-Asian cooperation for a venture which, without the Congo's invitation, would have seemed "neo-colonial." In comparable future situations, states may well prefer to take advantage of an intervention sponsored by the General Assembly, where an invitation is not a *carte blanche,* in preference to the services of the Security Council. Attractive as such an idea may sound, it should nevertheless be remembered that, had the United Nations had to act in the Congo on the basis of *consent,* it might well not have been able to act at all to prevent bloody civil war.

[55] See *supra* note 30.
[56] U.N. Doc. No. S/4389/Add.5. (Emphasis added.)

III

UNITED NATIONS JURISDICTION AND DOMESTIC JURISDICTION: THE LEGAL BASIS FOR INTERVENTION

In a sense, the world must thank God for the Belgians, for had they not intervened, the United Nations would certainly not have had so clear a jurisdictional basis for its interposition. The Belgians added the essential foreign ingredient which made the "situation" one of *international* peace and security as required by article thirty-nine of the United Nations Charter.

The original resolution of July 14, 1960, makes no reference to any particular authorizing paragraphs of the Charter, nor have subsequent resolutions done so. The Secretary General, however, has inclined to the view that "the Council's resolutions could be regarded as implicitly adopted under Article 40 and as based on an implicit finding under Article 39."[57] In any event, there is general agreement that no action authorized by the Security Council to date (with the possible contingent exception of one provision in the resolution of September 24, 1961)[58] could be regarded as an "enforcement measure" under chapter seven. Action under article forty is not such a measure but is, instead, comparable to a preliminary injunction. It is not an "enforcement measure" but a "provisional measure . . . without prejudice to the rights, claims or position of the parties concerned."[59]

This is not a purely academic difference. When the United Nations is engaged in an "enforcement measure" under chapter seven of the Charter, the fact that the object of such action ordinarily would be "essentially within the domestic jurisdiction" of the state where the action is taking place is not sufficient to bar the United Nations' right to act.[60] However, if—as in the overwhelming preponderance of ONUC activities—there is not the color of an "enforcement action," the United Nations must scrupulously avoid intervention in "matters which are essentially within the domestic jurisdiction" of any state.[61] This prohibition is not one to be waived even by the host state.[62] A United Nations action against a matter which is essentially domestic, if it is not of such gravity as to warrant an enforcement action, is *ultra vires*.

So long as the Belgian armed forces continued their incursion into Congolese territory, the United Nations was obviously not intervening in an "essentially

---

[57] ANNUAL REPORT 27. See also Miller, *Legal Aspects of the United Nations Action in the Congo*, 55 AM. J. INT'L L. 1, 4-9 (1961).

[58] U.N. Doc. No. S/5002. Paragraph 9 ". . . declares full and firm support for the Central Government of the Congo, and the determination to assist that Government in accordance with the decision of the United Nations to maintain law and order and national integrity, to provide technical assistance and to implement those decisions." What does "implement those decisions" mean? If "technical assistance" here means the same as in the first resolution (U.N. Doc. No. S/4387) it may be said to authorize the use of troops against rebels.

[59] U.N. CHARTER art. 40. See note 29 *supra*.
[60] *Id*. art. 2(7).   [61] *Ibid*.
[62] The Congolese Government has at times enacted laws which it then requests the ONUC to enforce. See, for example, the Ordinance of Aug. 24, 1961, concerning arrest of foreign mercenaries. U.N. Doc. No. S/4940/Add.14.

domestic" matter. However, once the Belgian troops were gone, the United Nations, still without engaging in an "enforcement action," began to intervene quite actively in a number of other matters which were not quite so obviously or so traditionally "international." Among these, the most important is the civil war with the provinces of Katanga and Orientale. It is not enough, say the critics, that the Congolese central government has in each instance requested United Nations help. It is beyond the powers of the United Nations to respond to such a request. It is this view which motivates French reaction to the Congo operation and which occasioned a French amendment to the resolution of December 20, 1961[63] asking the International Court to rule explicitly on whether the expenses incurred by ONUC were *ultra vires*.

What it comes to is this: May the United Nations decide to help one side of a civil war against another in the absence of a foreign military element? The vast preponderance of United Nations action has not, of course, been in the nature of such action. For one thing, it is only since the resolution of November 24, 1961, that the Security Council has specifically authorized it,[64] and then only to the ambiguous extent of rendering "technical assistance." Almost invariably, United Nations action has been motivated by the mandate to preserve "law and order" and to "prevent the occurrence of civil war."[65] In the case of United Nations military action against the Katanga Gendarmerie beginning on December 5, 1961, the expressed motivation was purely defensive. "This military action," the Acting Secretary General said,[66]

was undertaken with the greatest reluctance, and only when it became obvious that there was no use in continued negotiations.... The purpose of the present military operations is to regain and assure our freedom of movement, to restore law and order, and to ensure that for the future the United Nations forces and officials in Katanga are not subject to attacks; and meanwhile to react vigorously in self-defense to every assault on our present positions, by all the means available to us.

Similarly, Ambassador Stevenson has been at pains to explain that the "intention here has never been to interfere or to influence the political situation in the Congo.... The United Nations forces were attacked by Katanga forces in each case and this was a response to these attacks."[67] Nevertheless, the Secretary General has also placed the general position in a somewhat different perspective, noting his instructions that everything possible must be done to avert civil war. . . . This, I believe, *necessarily implies a sympathetic attitude on the part of ONUC towards the efforts of the Govern-*

[63] Resolution 1731 (XVI) on a report of the Fifth Committee, U.N. Doc. No. A/5062. This is the resolution asking for an advisory opinion on the legal status of special assessments in relation to article 17(a) of the Charter.
[64] U.N. Doc. No. S/5002. See also, however, Assembly Resolution 1474 (ES-IV), A/L.292/Rev./1, para. 2.
[65] U.N. Doc. No. Res. S/4741, para. 1.
[66] *The Congo—A Move Toward Reconciliation*, 9 U.N. Rev. 1, 7 (1962).
[67] *Hearings Before the Senate Comm. on Foreign Relations on S. 2768, Purchase of United Nations Bonds*, 87th Cong., 2d Sess. 89 (1962).

ment to suppress all armed activities against the Central Government and secessionist activities.[68]

A clearer example of United Nations intervention in a civil war situation than that afforded by the action in Katanga is the use of force on behalf of the Central Government against the regime in Orientale Province. Excerpts of the Report of the United Nations Officer in Charge are instructive:[69]

During the night of January 12-13 the Gendarmerie were mobilized and took position around Mr. Gizenga's residence and in their own camp (Camp Ketele). The Gendarmerie also erected roadblocks outside Mr. Gizenga's house and were reported to have arrested their own officers, who were being detained in Camp Ketele.

During the same night General Lundula's *Prevote militaire* and para-commandos took position around General Lundula's own headquarters.

In the morning of January 13 the President of the provincial government, Mr. Simon Losala, made a radio broadcast in which he indicated that Mr. Gizenga must leave Stanleyville and that the province would follow the Central Government. Mr. Gizenga was also told that he would have to take all the consequences in the event trouble broke out.

At approximately 9:00 o'clock in the morning of January 13 fighting broke out at Camp Ketele between the Gendarmerie and General Lundula's men which resulted in the death of eight gendarmes and six ANC soldiers. While the fight was going on, General Lundula requested that the United Nations should assist in restoring law and order by disarming the gendarmes.

Prime Minister Adoula was immediately informed of the fighting which had taken place and of the request for ONUC assistance submitted by General Lundula. . . .

The two letters were relayed immediately to the Acting Secretary-General who confirmed that the assistance requested by the Prime Minister could be afforded within the framework of ONUC's mandate to assist the Central Government in the maintenance of law and order and in the prevention of civil war. These instructions were conveyed to the ONUC Contingent Commander in Stanleyville in the evening of January 13. At that time, the ONUC troops in Stanleyville totalled some 980 men composed of the twenty-sixth Ethiopian battalion, a small detachment from the thirty-fifth Ethiopian battalion as well as various elements of an Ethiopian brigade command. Their Commanding Officer, Colonel Teshome, indicated that General Lundula had under his command five companies of ANC, two MP companies and two companies of para-commandos. The municipal police was also reported to be supporting General Lundula. The ONUC Contingent Commander was confident that there were thus sufficient troops to carry out the mandate, if required by developments in the situation.

A report received from the ONUC Chief Civilian Representative in Stanleyville indicated that on the morning of January 14 a conference had taken place in General Lundula's headquarters which was attended by a delegation from the gendarmes guarding Mr. Gizenga's residence and by ONUC representatives. The gendarmes were given thirty minutes by General Lundula to surrender and lay down their weapons. Accordingly, thirty-four gendarmes laid down their arms. During this conference, fighting was resumed at Camp Ketele and mortars were used. The fight lasted about half an hour and involved gendarmes and the soldiers of General Lundula.

[68] U.N. Doc. No. S/PV.892 at 71. (Emphasis added.)
[69] Report of the Officer-in-Charge of the United Nations Operation in the Congo to the Secretary-General, Jan. 20, 1962, U.N. Doc. No. 5/5053/Add.1 at 3-5.

The Gendarmerie Commander, one gendarmerie captain and a gendarmerie warrant officer, who had been arrested by their own troops, were liberated. They had been severely ill-treated and were taken immediately to the ONUC hospital.

Still in the morning of January 14, Mr. Gizenga, with whom the United Nations representatives were in close contact, requested ONUC to convey a telegram to the Prime Minister. . . .

During January 14 ONUC troops continued to assist those of General Lundula in disarming the Gendarmerie. By the end of the day the whole of the Gendarmerie, with the exception of approximately fifty men, had been disarmed. The ONUC military commander reported that during the whole operation only one ONUC platoon had been engaged which had not fired a single shot. Most of the prisoners were under ONUC protection, with the exception of one company which had stayed in its camp under ANC guard.

On the evening of January 14, General Lundula sent a message to Prime Minister Adoula.

On January 15 the joint operation of rounding up the remaining gendarmes was continued, and a further eighteen gendarmes were disarmed. Some of them were apprehended wearing civilian clothes. The situation in town was reported to be calm with ONUC troops continuing to enforce, in cooperation with General Lundula's troops, full security measures with respect to public law and order. In the afternoon of January 15th, Parliament in Leopoldville adopted the motion tabled on January 13th and thus endorsed the removal of Mr. Gizenga from his post of Vice-Prime Minister of the Central Government. Votes were cast as follows: sixty-seven for, one against, and four abstentions. . . .

Although the Stanleyville action, too, can be explained in terms of preserving "law and order" is is undisguisedly an intervention with decisive weight on the side of the central authorities in a situation of civil insurrection. Yet there is nothing particularly startling[70] about the proposition that the jurisdiction of the United Nations extends to such an intervention and that a civil war, although fought entirely in the Congo by Congolese, may still involve consequences not "essentially domestic" in their effect. The United Nations continues to be engaged in an interposition in the Congo, although it is no longer primarily one against an actual invasion such as faced UNEF, or ONUC during its inception. It has instead become an interposition against domestic forces which carry into a purely domestic war the talismans, the aspirations, and the indirect support of parties to the "cold war." It is an interposition against foreign "volunteers" who in the Congo, as in Korea, provided the brains and brawn of the conflict. It is an interposition against foreign economic interests which provide the financing for insurrection. Most important, it is an interposition against a chaos which, if allowed to go unchecked, would have made the direct interposition of cold-war forces inevitable.

This constitutes a notable, but sensible and historically consistent diminution of the meaning of "domestic jurisdiction" as used in article 2(7) of the Charter.

---

[70] Cf. 1 L. OPPENHEIM, INTERNATIONAL LAW 290-94 (8th ed., Lauterpacht 1955), and especially the discussion of the Trail Smelter Arbitration of 1938, at 291 n.2. Also Emperor of Austria v. Day and Kossuth, 2 Giff. 628, 66 Eng. Rep. 263 (V.C. 1861).

There are two other bases on which United Nations jurisdiction has been invoked to restrict freedom of action of Congolese authorities. On two occasions, once in September 1960, when Lumumbist Lulua troops slaughtered one thousand Kasai Balubas, and again, when in March 1961, the Lunda troops of President Tshombe launched their massive attack on the Katanga Balubas, the United Nations Command justified intervention by invoking, *inter alia,* the Genocide Convention.[71] This is of particular importance to the development of United Nations law, since hostility between tribes is one of the more omnipresent shadows lingering over much of newly-independent Africa.

Finally, the United Nations has, on a number of occasions, intervened in otherwise "domestic" matters to uphold human rights and fundamental freedoms.[72] In February 1961, Ambassador Dayal on this basis intervened with the Gizenga authorities in Stanleyville against a proposed $600 levy on every Belgian male over the age of twenty-one. The same authority, supplementing the "law and order" mandate, was cited to justify the establishment of neutral or "protected" areas in the towns, and to grant protection and asylum to political refugees—even, on occasion, in defiance of arrest warrants issued by the Central Government.[73]

IV

THE UNITED NATIONS AND CONSTITUTIONAL LAW

Right from the start of its intervention, ONUC faced the collapse of constitutional government in the Congo. On Monday, July 11, 1960, the Katanga legislature proclaimed its independence and secession, demanding diplomatic recognition and admission to the United Nations. In dealing with this alleged "right of self-determination" the task of the United Nations was substantially simplified by the fact that not one state has extended diplomatic recognition to Katanga. The United Nations Operation followed the unanimous precedent of the member states in refusing to treat the Tshombe government as sovereign. In this it was supported by article six of the *Loi fondamentale,* which specifically forbids secession. It was also supported by the legal circumstances which surround the formation of the Tshombe government. Articles 110 and 114 of the *Loi* had emerged from the pre-independence Round Table Conference with an agreed provision making a two-thirds quorum in provincial assemblies prerequisite to the election of provincial governments. The outcome of the Katangese provincial election had, however, given M. Tshombe a parliamentary following of only twenty-four to twenty-two for the

---

[71] ANNUAL REPORT 11 and 35. For text of the Genocide Convention, see Resolution No. 260 (III), Gen. Ass. Off. Rec. Res. at 1744, U.N. Doc. No. A/810.

[72] See International Declaration of Human Rights adopted by the General Assembly on Dec. 10, 1948, U.N. Doc. No. A/810, at 71.

[73] ANNUAL REPORT 41. For description of the protection given to M. Lumumba, see Report of the Commission on Investigation, Nov. 11, 1961, U.N. Doc. No. A/4964 at 13-16; also Second Progress Report to the Secretary-General from his Special Representative, Nov. 2, 1960, U.N. Doc. No. S/4557, in SECURITY COUNCIL OFF. REC. 15th year, Supp. Oct.-Dec. 1960, at 12.

Opposition Balubakat party (with thirteen Tshombe-inclined Independents). By boycotting the provincial sittings, Balubakat was able to prevent the lawful election of M. Tshombe's government. Thereupon, two weeks before independence, Belgium unilaterally took it upon itself to repeal the two-thirds quorum provision.[74]

Therefore, the legal status of Katangese independence is not without blemish. This fact alone could not, however, be conclusive for ONUC. The right of revolution, of "self-determination," is obviously not primarily subject to the standard of domestic legality. Neither, however, is it an absolute right in international law. The Austrian State Treaty, for example, specifically forbids Austria to "self-determine" itself into union with Germany.[75] The United Nations has similarly refused to support cultural autonomy for the people of Alto-Adige and, more significantly, has specifically rejected self-determination as a course of development for the Ewe tribe of the British Togoland Trusteeship.[76] The concept of "self-determination," which is merely one of the purposes of the United Nations, co-exists, for example, with respect for "territorial integrity"[77] as well as with "political, economic, social and educational advancement."[78] In practice, the United Nations has with consistency opposed the formation of small, economically unviable entities—the most recent example being the efforts exerted by the World Organization to prevent the total separation of the Kingdoms of Ruanda and Urundi.[79]

In the case of Katanga, the impact which secession would have on the political, economic, social and educational advancement of the Congo as a whole may best be judged by the fact that one Katangese corporation, the Union Minière du Haut Katanga, before independence supplied the central exchequer of the Congo with approximately one third its tax revenues, and even in 1960, continued to pay some $52 million in taxes and dividends to the government.[80] United Nations jurisprudence has developed a consistent practice of limiting the "right" of self-determination to overseas[81] colonial possessions and to instances in which independence is economically and socially feasible. It is in this light that one must read the Security Council's eloquent resolution of November 24, 1961, where it declares that "all secessionist activities against the Republic of the Congo are contrary to the *Loi fondamentale* and Security Council decisions" and "specifically *demands* that such activities which are now taking place in Katanga shall cease forthwith."[82]

A much more difficult legal problem arose out of the disintegration of the central government of the Congo. The United Nations intervention had been authorized

---

[74] REPUBLIC OF THE CONGO, MINISTRY OF FOREIGN AFFAIRS, DOCUMENT DIVISION, THE PROVINCE OF KATANGA AND CONGOLESE INDEPENDENCE 9-11 (1962).

[75] State Treaty for the Re-establishment of an Independent and Democratic Austria, 217 U.N.T.S. 225 (1955).

[76] An abridged account of the lengthy considerations preceding the decision to reject the Ewe claim may be found in LOUIS B. SOHN, CASES AND MATERIALS ON UNITED NATIONS LAW 742-72 (1956).

[77] U.N. CHARTER art. 2(4).   [78] *Id.* art. 73(a).

[79] See *A Formula for Ruanda-Urundi*, 9 U.N. REV. 6 (1962). See also *id.* at 63.

[80] N.Y. Times, Dec. 12, 1961.

[81] U.N. Doc. No. A/4526, Part V(B).   [82] U.N. Doc. No. S/5002.

to supply military assistance to "the Government of the Congo" and to do so "in consultation with the Government of the Congo."[83] The entire operation predicated a cooperative venture between the ONUC and a legally-constituted and accepted Central Government of the Congo. When on September 5, 1960, such a government ceased to exist, the United Nations, having already committed some 18,000 officers and men from twenty-nine nations to the ONUC undertaking, were placed in an unexpectedly awkward position.[84] *Which* "Government of the Congo" was to be assisted, *whose* "law and order" was to be enforced, *what* "national security" was to be maintained?

In this case, the United Nations could not rely upon purely behaviorist international law. Some nations, after the fall of Premier Lumumba, extended recognition to the government of his vice-Premier, Gizenga, at Stanleyville: among them the communist nations of Eastern Europe, as well as Morocco, Mali, Cuba, Ghana, Outer Mongolia, Guinea, Yugoslavia, Indonesia, and Ceylon. Other states maintained relations with the regime at Léopoldville, and India maintained diplomatic relations with neither.[85] Whereas in the case of non-recognition of Katanga, ONUC could observe and follow the consistent behavior of its member states, there was no such clear guidance to help it sort out the problem of the rival central governments.

It therefore became necessary for the United Nations, relying on its "law and order" mandate, to develop a certain expertise in Congolese constitutional law in order to interpret the legality of the events following the dismissal by President Kasavubu on September 5 of his Prime Minister, Lumumba. According to the *Loi fondamentale*,[86] the "Government of the Congo is composed of the Prime Minister and the Ministers."[87] It specifically does *not* include the President who, as Chief of State, is a separate "institution."[88] On the other hand, the "Chief of State designates and revokes the Prime Minister and his Ministers"[89] but if, as occurred on September 5, the Chief of State does discharge the Government, a new one must present itself to Parliament for a vote of confidence.[90] Between the time of M. Lumumba's dismissal and the vote of confidence given by the reassembled Parliament to the Government of M. Adoula,[91] no constitutional government functioned in the Congo.[92] There was, in other words, a governmental interregnum of eleven months.

[83] Resolution of July 14, 1960, U.N. Doc. No. S/4387.
[84] Second Progress Report, U.N. Doc. No. S/4557, at 26.
[85] N.Y. Times, Feb. 19, 1961, § 1, p. 1, col. 7; p. 14, cols. 1-7.
[86] Law of May 19, 1960; [1960] MONITEUR BELGE 3988. This law had not, incidentally, been subject to adoption as a national constitution by the Congolese Parliament and was therefore itself only the "best thing available" for assessing the legalities of the constitutional crisis.
[87] Loi fondamentale art. 35.   [88] *Id*. art. 8, *lit*. a.
[90] *Id*. art. 42.   [91] U.N. Doc. No. S/4913, at 2.
[92] The United Nations was not only faced with the delicate task of interpreting the *Loi fondamentale* but also of political events which purported to bear on that interpretation. Thus, on Sept. 14, for example, the Congolese Parliament held its last session before the interregnum, a joint meeting at which "full powers" were voted to M. Lumumba. According to the ONUC Special Representative, however, the decision "was somewhat uncertain as to both substance and count." ANNUAL REPORT 13. The

What was the position of ONUC during this period towards Congolese legal authority? There was, of course, no shortage of contenders for the position vacated by M. Lumumba. First, President Kasavubu named Joseph Ileo to head a new Government. On September 14, 1960, Col. Mobutu announced the suspension of constitutional government, and that "in view of the struggle going on between two opposing governments,"[93] a *collège d'universitaires* would take charge of the management of the ministerial departments. The appointment of these "Commissioners General" was ratified by presidential decree on September 20, but the earlier presidential decree designating a government under M. Ileo was never rescinded.[94] Furthermore, Colonel Mobutu let it be known that he objected to the President's participation in legitimizing his Government, as he had "neutralized political personalities."[95]

During most of the ensuing period the Mobutu government was never able to extend its control much beyond a 70-mile perimeter around Léopoldville. Twenty-six officers of the Congolese National Army, who were sent on a mission of reconciliation to the six provinces, were ultimately discharged from the army without completing the mission on the ground that they had been "indoctrinated" in the course of carrying it out.[96] Meanwhile, M. Lumumba, who continued to occupy the residence of the Prime Minister, surrounded by concentric rings of ONUC and ANC troops, showed up the tenuous control of Colonel Mobutu even in Léopoldville by emerging on occasion to make tours of the city or to hold a press conference. After his attempted escape, M. Lumumba was transferred to the maximum security of the Thysville ANC barracks, but even here he was reportedly soon enjoying the run of the camp and indoctrinating the troops. This led to the former Premier's fateful further transfer to Katanga.

An earlier Secretary-General had, in a legal memorandum, defined a test for deciding whether to accredit the United Nations delegates of a government whose status was in doubt:[97]

The question at issue should be which of these ... governments in fact is in a position to employ the resources and direct the people of the state in fulfillment of the obligations of membership. In essence, this means an inquiry as to whether the government exercises effective authority within the territory of the state and is habitually obeyed by the bulk of the population.

Obviously, this does not describe the authority of any government in the Congo, including that of Colonel Mobutu, during the interregnum.

New York Times reported the Secretary-General as declaring that, according to eye witnesses, "in the hall of the Chamber of Deputies there were some scores of the ANC [army] present—then loyal to Mr. Lumumba—during the debate and voting. They were fully armed with rifles and sub-machine guns." N.Y. Times, Dec. 14, 1960, p. 1, cols. 6-7.

[93] Second Interim Report of the Special Representative, U.N. Doc. No. S/4557, at 10.
[94] *Id.* at 11.   [95] *Ibid.*   [96] *Ibid.*
[97] Memorandum prepared by the Secretary-General, February 1950, SECURITY COUNCIL OFF. REC. 5th year, Supp. Jan.-May 1950 (S/1466) at 18-23 (1950).

The United Nations acted in accordance with this formula. "Committed to the principle of neutrality, it could not have chosen between rival governments, nor could it respond to the continuing appeals that it install one or another government."[98] Committed to the principle of "law and order," it could not give full *de jure* recognition to the perpetrators of a military coup. On the other hand, it was quite prepared to establish *de facto* relations with Colonel Mobutu's Government in so far as it exercised *de facto* control. Ambassador Dayal laid down the policy:[99]

ONUC . . . while taking no position on the legality of the constitutional decree-law of October 11, 1960 creating the Council of Commissioners-General, has continued to follow its policy of dealing, in routine matters, with whatever authority it finds in the ministerial chairs.

It also continued to recognize the legal position of M. Kasavubu as Head of State[100] and Colonel Mobutu as Chief of Staff[101]—matters about which there was little legal controversy.

On the other hand, in areas which were clearly not within the *de facto* control of the Mobutu government, the United Nations carried on technical relations with whatever authority *was* in control,[102] meanwhile bending every effort to bring about national reconciliation by means of reconvening Parliament and promoting the election of a truly national government.

That was accomplished, with the United Nations providing the essential safeguards,[103] on July 22, 1961.

[98] Second Progress Report of the Special Representative, U.N. Doc. No. S/4557, at 14.
[99] *Ibid.*   [100] *Ibid.*   [101] *Ibid.*
[102] For example, Exchange of Messages Between the Secretary-General and Mr. Tshombe, U.N. Doc. No. S/4557, Annex B.
[103] U.N. Doc. No. S/4841.